Reading History

A Practical Guide to Improving Literacy

Reading History

A Practical Guide to Improving Literacy

by

Janet Allen

with

Christine Landaker

OXFORD
UNIVERSITY PRESS

OXFORD

UNIVERSITY PRESS

Oxford   New York

Auckland Bangkok Buenos Aires Cape Town Chennai
Dar es Salaam Delhi Hong Kong Istanbul Karachi Kolkata
Kuala Lumpur Madrid Melbourne Mexico City Mumbai
Nairobi São Paulo Shanghai Taipei Tokyo Toronto

Copyright © 2005 by Oxford University Press, Inc.

Published by Oxford University Press, Inc.
198 Madison Avenue, New York, New York, 10016
http://www.oup.com/us

Oxford is a registered trademark of Oxford University Press

Library of Congress Cataloging-in-Publication Data

Allen, Janet, 1950-
Reading history : strategies to improve comprehension and
connections in social studies classes / Janet Allen with Christine Landaker.
p. cm.
Includes bibliographical references.
ISBN 0-19-516595-0 (cloth) — ISBN 0-19-516596-9 (pbk.)
1. Content area reading. 2. Social sciences—Study and teaching (Middle school)
I. Landaker, Christine. II. Title.
LB1050.455.A43 2004
428.4′07′12—dc22
2004017141

1   3   5   7   9   8   6   4   2
Printed in the United States of America

Oxford University Press gratefully acknowledges those who permitted
the use of the following materials in copyright:

Billy Collins, "The History Teacher." In *Sailing Alone around the Room: New and Selected Poems.*
New York: Random House, Inc., 2002.

Sara Holbrook, "Naked." In *Chicks Up Front.* Cleveland: Cleveland State University Poetry Center, 1998.
Reprinted with permission of Sara Holbrook.

The History Teacher

Trying to protect his students' innocence
he told them the Ice Age was really just
the Chilly Age, a period of a million years
when everyone had to wear sweaters.

And the Stone Age became the Gravel Age,
named after the long driveways of the time.

The Spanish Inquisition was nothing more
than an outbreak of questions such as
"How far is it from here to Madrid?"
"What do you call the matador's hat?"

The War of the Roses took place in a garden,
and the Enola Gay dropped one tiny atom on Japan.

The children would leave his classroom
for the playground to torment the weak
and the smart,
mussing up their hair and breaking their glasses,

while he gathered up his notes and walked home
past flower beds and white picket fences,
wondering if they would believe that soldiers
in the Boer War told long, rambling stories
designed to make the enemy nod off.

Billy Collins

Contents

"The Silver War" and Other Challenges to Reading History

To be literate in content classrooms, students must learn how to use language processes to explore and construct meaning with texts. When students put language to work for them in content classrooms, it helps them to discover, organize, retrieve, and elaborate on what they are learning.

Richard T. Vacca (2000, 16)

Many of us cringe as we hear or read another story of students telling us historical facts that leave us stunned: Robin Williams discovered Rhode Island, and King Henry VIII is friends with Prince Charles because they've both been divorced. We know that these bits of misinformation come from the students' lack of meaningful connection to the history they have studied. However, as we struggle to cover all the required course content, we often give students glimpses of history that are neither meaningful nor memorable. During a similar event in my classroom, I became acutely aware of the impact of inadequate background knowledge on the reading task.

I always began class with a brief read-aloud. On this day, I had chosen to read Maya Angelou's poem "No Losers, No Weepers." Just before class began, I discovered that we had a set of *Reading Road to Writing* workbooks, which contained a brief biography of Angelou's life. Thinking that the students might have a more substantive connection to the poem if they had some knowledge of the poet, I proceeded to read the biographical information to them, before reading the poem. When I finished reading the short biography,

I asked them some questions to clarify what we had just read. The transcript of my class that day gives a clear picture of the contrast between telling students "stuff" and actively involving them in building background knowledge for reading (Allen 1995, 113–114).

Janet: What do you think they're talking about when they say, "She did what her ancestors could only wish for?"
Melvin: She freed the slaves.
Janet: Did we have slaves when Maya Angelou lived?
Tammy: No.
Janet: When did we have slaves?
Mac: With Columbus?
Terri: In the 1500s?
Derek: 1700s.
Tanya: World War II.

By this point I was becoming more exasperated than I wanted to admit and the class was in pandemonium.

Janet: Wait. . . . Stop. . . .What war was fought to get rid of slavery?
Tori: World War II.
Diana: World War I.
Mac: Revolutionary War.
Janet: This is pathetic. What war was fought over slavery?
Melvin: The Silver War.

This wasn't horseshoes; close was good enough.

Janet: That's close, Melvin. The Civil War. Now, who was president at this time?
Terri: Abraham Lincoln.

A smart teacher would have stopped there; I finally had a right answer.

Janet: Great, now we're getting somewhere. Now, what two parts of the country were fighting?
Tanya: England and the West.
Janet: Now, let's try and get these facts straight.
Tammy: Just tell us if it's a, b, or c. It's a, right?
Janet: The point is not whether it's a, b, or c; the point is learning something. This needs to make sense.
Tammy: It would make sense if we just wrote down the right answer.

Anne: I know the answer. The Civil War was fought between the North and the South.

Mac: I thought that was the Revolution War.

Janet: What was the Revolutionary War fought for?

Diane: Freedom.

Janet: For whom?

Tori: Jews?

Melvin: Blacks?

Mac: Italians?

Janet: Arghh!

When I transcribed my class notes later that day, it occurred to me how often students are asked to read and write about concepts, themes, and events about which they have no working knowledge. On reflection, I was able to see that I myself was an additional problem because I wasn't building background knowledge that day; I was simply asking my students to regurgitate bits of information that clearly had no meaning to them. It was a perfect lesson for me on the difference between giving information and building meaningful background knowledge that will support reading, writing, and research.

While these kinds of stored "facts" will probably always plague us, the quotation from Vacca highlights the value in using reading and writing in history classes. Those processes help students think more clearly about content, extend and demonstrate new understandings about their learning, and expand their academic vocabularies. Yet, for the past several years, many history teachers have voiced a common complaint about getting their students to do any content reading: "My students just can't or won't read their texts for my classes. Students complain that the books are too difficult and boring. They seem to want to be entertained all of the time." If this scenario sounds familiar to you, then you are trying to overcome the same challenges many of us face.

Understanding the Challenges of Reading History

As we teach and learn with a generation of children who have been raised on technology and sophisticated media, it becomes increasingly difficult to entice them into reading content texts. Yet, when I think back to my days as a student, I have to admit that I experienced the same attitudes and difficulties students express today: boredom, lack of motivation, confusion, frustration, anxiety, helplessness, hopelessness, and, in some cases, failure. One difference between my experience and those of our students today is that it wasn't acceptable for me not to do the work just because I was bored. Whether I was engaged or not, I was expected to complete assignments, pass exams, and participate in class. These expectations may not have increased my engagement with the reading, but they certainly increased my chances for successful completion of those classes. In spite of a lack of engagement with reading history, I had enough skill as a reader to decode most of the assigned reading and a fairly complex network of strategies and resources for overcoming the difficulties of the assigned text.

For many students, their disinterest in reading history is characterized by several roadblocks to success. These roadblocks include a lack of interest and motivation, classroom resources that are insufficient or inappropriate for their reading levels, the absence of instructional support that would help them learn to read complex texts, insufficient background knowledge, an inability to break the code of the textbook, and a lack of independent reading and research strategies. When students face so many challenges, they fail at reading history and in the process may also cause classroom management issues.

At a time of high-stakes testing, standards-based assessment, curriculum alignment, and budget deficits, most of us seem caught between "nonstandard kids and a killing curriculum" (Ohanian 2001). As money for engaging resources decreases and the demand for content knowledge increases, many teachers are depending on the textbook as a primary source for classroom instruction. Even proficient readers can experience failure under these conditions, and struggling readers simply refuse to make the attempt. The difficulties these students face because of their lack of background knowledge for the content, their inability to negotiate the supports and challenges of academic texts, or their unfamiliarity with specialized content vocabulary make both the teaching and learning of history overwhelming.

We have all experienced the teaching difficulties that arise when students are overwhelmed with reading and writing tasks that seem impossible for them. In *What Really Matters for Struggling Readers*, Richard Allington makes the connection between reading tasks that are too challenging and students' behavior: "Students given tasks where success was low were far more likely to cease work on the task and engage in nonacademic behaviors than were students working at high success rates. Thus, many classroom management difficulties were linked to the relative difficulty of school work students were given" (2001, 45). Christine Landaker, a middle school social studies teacher who collaborated with me in writing this book, describes her experience with this dynamic in her classroom.

Two years ago, I had an eighth-grade class that was the most challenging group of students I have ever taught. The characteristics students exhibited in relation to reading and learning history were often the same. "This is boring" was the rampant refrain before we ever started anything. They came to me with a lack of success on all fronts, mostly from traditional lecture/textbook classes where they had to gain most of their knowledge from reading a textbook that bored them and was too difficult. Then, they had to answer questions that were literal level and required no thought, simply finding the catchphrase in the text. They saw no relevance to their lives or in what had happened in the past. Anything that didn't immediately and intimately affect them wouldn't hold their interest. Even the attack on the World Trade Center was old news by the second day. They just didn't talk about it. It was over and done; move on. That was pretty much how they treated history.

Most of us have had these years in the classroom. Classes like this always left me feeling like a failure, and Christine experienced those same feelings. It wasn't until I began to figure out that the apathy and disinterest students exhibited each day were actually survival tools used to make up for a history of failure and frustration that I could begin to figure out some instructional strategies that would help them find more success. This book highlights those strategies that helped our students become successful readers of history.

When Christine surveyed her middle school students this year, we knew we were starting from a better foundation. In spite of the reading difficulties students highlighted when they were given lots of textbook reading assignments, these students enjoyed and learned from certain aspects of reading history.

If you know history, you know your future.
History allows us to know about the world and our past.
History helps us understand our own history.
History repeats itself.
History allows us to know and understand war.
History prepares us for our future—for jobs like being an anthropologist.
Knowing history can make the world a better place.

In their own way, these students summarized the importance of reading history: to learn from our mistakes, to translate historical truths into lessons for our lives, to see where we have come from, and to know that we are connected in infinite ways. The reasons for reading history were so compelling that only two students believed schools should not require social studies classes.

Students believed that reading history is important, but they were also quick to point out which instructional methods made reading history interesting and worth studying and which made it difficult and uninteresting.

Positive Practices	Negative Practices
Projects	Sitting and taking notes
Learning about ancient times	Studying boring current events
Study games for review	Vocabulary tests
Traveling around the world	Homework that is too hard
Learning interesting facts	Boring worksheets
Working on group projects	Silent reading
Shared reading (read-alouds)	Doing book work
Learning about prejudice	Too much answering questions
Doing activities	Reading and answering questions

Finally, these students had a purpose for reading history: they had questions for which they were hoping to find answers. Some questions, such as Eduardo's, were inappropriate, but not unexpected: "Was Hitler gay or just stupid?" However, the following small sample of their questions demonstrates the range and depth of their thinking. In fact, many of us wonder about these questions every day.

Has religion caused wars?
Has anyone found the lost city of Atlantis?
Were there ever wars that made a difference?
Why do we have wars?
Why can't people/countries get along?
Who killed Dr. Martin Luther King?
Why does Bin Laden hate the United States?
Where do traditions come from?

In this book, Christine and I have listened to these students' words—to their insights, their reflections, and their questions—in order to design curriculum and instruction. We have not viewed social studies standards as content to be covered; rather, we have used them as a frame for designing curriculum, instruction, and assessment that is meaningful and memorable.

In chapter 1, we highlight a variety of instructional strategies for assessing and building background knowledge. These strategies often help decrease the number of "Silver War" events you might have in your classroom. In chapter 2, we describe methods for supporting and monitoring comprehension.

Instructional strategies for helping students read their textbooks as well as other informational and historical texts are explored. In chapter 3, we examine a variety of ways to assess and extend the content knowledge your students have gained from reading history, providing a range of assessment and evaluation tools. The final chapter synthesizes the practices we believe increase both academic achievement and student interest in reading history.

Finally, the appendices provide additional resources with which you can supplement textbooks. Christine has provided annotations of her favorite professional books (Appendix B), Web sites (Appendix E), and resources (Appendix C), as well as extensive sets of texts to support thematic or unit-based instruction in social studies (Appendix D). We have also included blank copies of all graphic organizers used throughout the book so that you may use them with your students (Appendix A). While every instructional strategy we describe may not be appropriate for you and your students, it is our hope that the support offered by these methods will help your students begin to see history as somebody's story—a story they will want to read again and again.

Chapter 1

Building Foundations for Reading Success

Pre-Reading Strategies for Assessing and Building Background Knowledge

> We are addicted to coverage. This addiction seems endemic in high schools . . . but it affects all levels of the curriculum, from kindergarten through college. We expose students to broad surveys of the disciplines and to endless sets of skills and competencies. . . the press for broad coverage causes many teachers to feel inadequate about leaving out so much content and apologetically mindful of the fact that much of what they teach is not fully understood by their students.
>
> F. M. Newman (1988)

At a time when districts have mandated coverage of elaborate lists of content standards, most teachers are feeling the challenge of covering so much material with students who come to class lacking the interest, background knowledge or content language necessary for reading historical texts. An additional challenge affects our instructional decisions when we also must work with students who have no sense of the time and place in which they live. Christine's 8th grade classroom offers us a great example of how difficult it is to teach, or even to know where to begin, when this combination of problems occurs.

Christine and her students had just begun a unit on Colonial America, and Christine worked with her students to generate a list of information they would need to find in order to be experts on what life was like in one of the three Colonial regions. After generating their lists, students used three sources to create their descriptions of life in Colonial America: *A History of*

US, the district-adopted textbooks, and related supplemental trade books. Imagine Christine's surprise when one group of experts reported that colonists traveled by whores and communicated via cell phones! On days like this, we are reminded of how important it is to build background knowledge with students before asking them to read, write, or conduct research.

Activating and Building Background Knowledge

Even our best students struggle to understand concepts that seem far removed from their lives, and our most struggling readers are often so overwhelmed they do not even attempt to read their assignments. As content teachers, we have four broad tasks:

- Assessing the knowledge base students bring to the study
- Providing students with experiences that give them a rich and memorable context for their reading
- Anticipating words and concepts that may make reading difficult
- Helping students develop questions they would like to answer so that they have a purpose for reading

Assessing Students' Background Knowledge

As we were writing this book, Christine reminded me just how important it is simply to ask students what they already know—before beginning teaching. She said she often starts class by writing the following statement on the board: "What do you already know or think you know about _____?" She then records students' answers on a chart or transparency. They then revisit these "facts" throughout their course of study, modifying their contributions with new information as they discover it. When the class studied the *Mayflower*, a lot of students at first thought it was one of Columbus's ships. As they sorted through how so many students come to have the same misinformation, Christine finally figured out that many of them had been in elementary classes where a unit on the Pilgrims was always taught after a unit on Columbus; the students had simply blended the two units in their memories.

In the process of such fact-finding, Christine is able to plan instruction that builds on what students bring, providing opportunities for them to verify information or replace misinformation, and to help students place information in accurate historical context. This assessment then leads her to the three remaining instructional goals: creating meaningful contexts, anticipating and using content language, and developing questions to guide reading.

Creating Meaningful and Memorable Historical Contexts

In "Reading Interests of High School Students," Diaz-Rubin highlights the importance of meaningful and memorable contexts for reading: "Learning occurs when the student perceives an importance between the material being presented and his life or world" (1996, 169–170). Taking the time to uncover, rather than cover, history means that we have to plan carefully for activities that will create a bridge between students' lives and interests and the content that we have chosen for them to study.

While "colonists traveling with cell phones" is an unsettling example of a gap in historical context, it also reminds us how critical it is to build a context with our students prior to extensive reading. This can be done using a variety of approaches. One approach that seems to immediately engage students is the use of artifacts. In Christine's classroom, she often creates and gives to the students boxes of artifacts with which study groups can construct a context for the time period and events.

Prior to student reading and research related to the Civil War, Christine created a box filled with primary source documents. Students worked in study groups to examine the documents in order to build context for the time, people, and surrounding events. The following questions helped guide students through the documents so that they could pose their own questions, make predictions and inferences, and document information.

1. What is the oldest document in the collection? How do you know?
2. Which is the "newest" document in the collection? How do you know?
3. Look at the clothing catalog. Read pp. 2–3, 5 (have someone read the poem out loud), 9, 30–31. How is this catalog similar to today's clothing catalog? How is it different? What do you learn about people's lives from looking at the clothing catalog? What year is the catalog dated?
4. Skim over the other documents tucked inside the catalog. What are they? What do they tell you about life in the South during the Civil War?
5. Look at the documents tucked inside the "List of the Names of the Enlisted Men." Someone read aloud the letter on purple paper (pp. 11–13 of the guide for the easy-to-read version). Why do you think the letter

writer knew he was dying? What are the other documents, and what do they tell you about the battles and the military during the Civil War?

6. Use the stereo glasses (Take turns!) to look at the 3-D pictures. Study the other pictures, too. Make sure to read any writing on the front and back of the pictures. What questions do you have after looking at all of them?

7. Independent Question (This means you do this one by yourself.): What did you learn about the Civil War from looking through the documents? What questions do you have about this time in history?

When students finished examining the documents, they each created a web to document what they had learned about people, places, events, and causes of the Civil War. Anthony can use the initial web he created to represent his discoveries (see Figure 1.1) to record additional information he learns about the Civil War in the course of the reading and inquiry the class will do during the unit.

Providing students with a wide variety of reading materials is another way Christine helps her students become engaged in reading history. She always provides them with access to primary source documents, nonfiction, fiction, poetry, other students' writing, photographs, picture books and periodicals for reading, small-group activities, research, and clarification of questions. When James Cameron's *Titanic* came out, Christine capitalized on the phenomenon to show her students they could make personal connections to historical times, places, people, and events.

> As teachers, we always try to make history come alive for our students. Never was the opportunity easier than the year James Cameron's *Titanic* was released. We studied the Titanic as part of a unit on Europe and immigration so students could see the larger context for this event. The movie was followed by many books based on the ship, her passengers, and life at the beginning of the twentieth century. I decided to capitalize on this opportunity and have my seventh graders "sail" on the ship. I collected the names, ages, cities of origin and destination, and ship's class of one passenger for each of my students. I allowed them to draw names out of a hat and each student then became that passenger for the duration of the unit.
>
> On the final day of the unit, we had a shipboard meal of shepherd's pie since we were all in third class that day. After our meal, each of the students learned his/her passenger's fate. Ebony had been Mathilde Lefebre, an 11-year-old girl traveling from France with her family. When I came to her name, I could see Ebony's lip trembling. As I calmly stated,

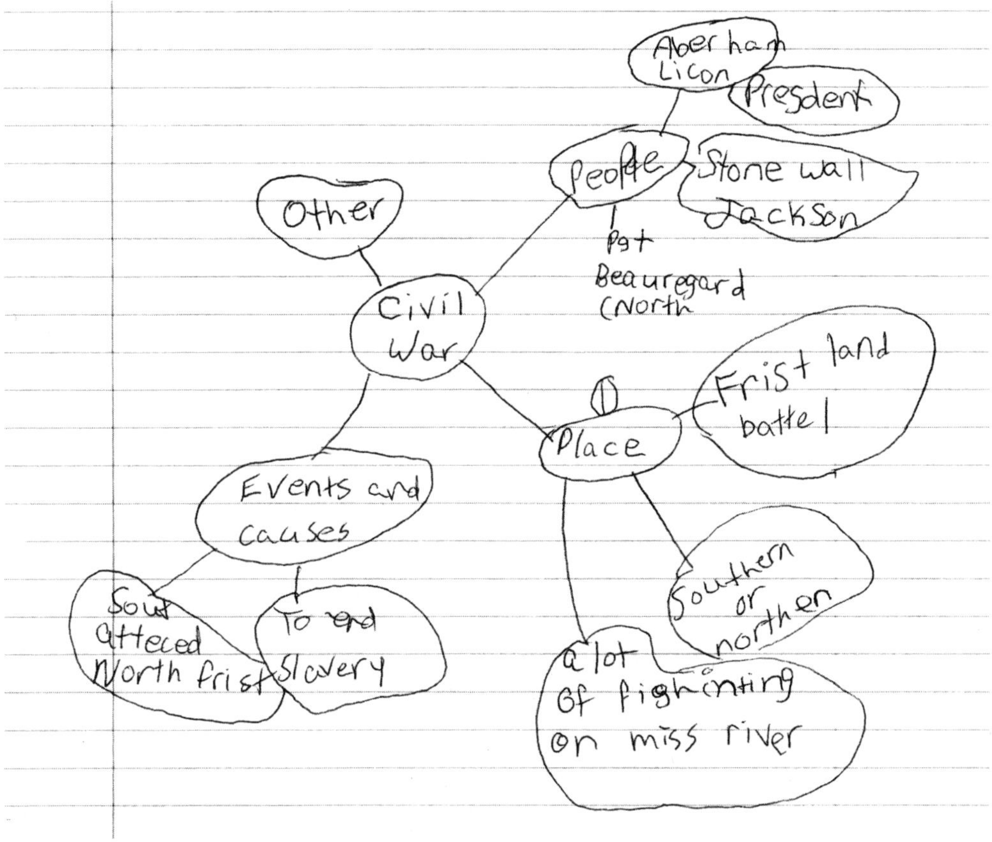

Figure 1.1 Anthony's Documentation Web

"Mathilde Lefebre, lost at sea with her family," Ebony burst into tears. "I knew it. I just knew it. She was so young, and she was so nice, and she and her whole family were going to start over again. I just knew none of them would make it."

Ebony could not be consoled and so during the evening I called home to make sure her mother understood what had happened. Her mother's response was a good reminder to me of the value of helping our students make strong and powerful connections to history. "You know, Ms. Landaker, I'm not upset that you made my daughter cry. I'm just happy that you helped her make a connection to history like that. She has talked about nothing except the *Titanic* and Mathilde for the past two weeks."

In this example, Christine has brought her students into reading history by providing them with rich resources they would want to read. She gave all her students access to common texts by reading them aloud as students followed along (shared reading). Each time she begins a new unit, she follows a similar format, using a wide variety of texts to get students engaged in the study. These texts have the additional value of helping students build content-specific word banks that support reading, writing, and research as well as fostering questions they would like to answer during the unit of learning. Appendix D has many examples of the text sets Christine uses for various time periods and themes.

Of course, making history meaningful is only one aspect of assessing and building background knowledge. In order to make history memorable, we have to employ a variety of instructional strategies and activities that support connecting, organizing, analyzing, and synthesizing the information students have encountered with these texts. I am sure there are hundreds of activities that would serve the dual purposes of assessing and building background knowledge, but we discovered several that we have returned to multiple times because of our success with their use: Admits Slips, Book Pass, Here and Now, Skimming and Scanning, and Writing to Learn.

Admit Slips

A significant amount of research has documented the impact of activating a reader's schema prior to reading (McKeown et al. 1991; Vygotsky 1962). When we take the time to activate and add to a reader's background knowledge (schema) prior to reading or study, we front-load support for their study. This background knowledge makes them better able to find information, answer questions, and make connections between reading, their lives, and other texts, as well as meeting assessment or evaluation purposes. Admit Slips usually consist of small amounts of reading combined with an opportunity for students to make connections and predictions or generate questions for content that will be studied the following day. When they are given as homework, many students come to class prepared for and interested in the content.

I find more students will do Admit Slips as homework if the admit slip can be put on a single sheet of paper. The Admit Slip shown in Figure 1.2 uses a copy of pages 83–85 from *All the People: 1945–2001* (*A History of US*, Book 10) as a way to assess and build background knowledge prior to beginning a unit on the Civil Rights Movement. The prompts on the Admit Slip ask students to read the text, examine title and headings, and use the strategies of predicting, inferring and questioning to examine and anticipate content. Because the Admit Slip is not so daunting as being asked to read an entire

16 Three Boys and Six Girls

Some white children in segregated schools wanted to try integration. "They don't want you to think for yourself," said one Central High student. "Let us try it. Make the parents go home." But others, like those above, needed to learn about fairness—and about spelling, too.

The fight to see that all Americans—black, white, Hispanic, Asian, female—would be treated fairly was called the **"civil rights movement."** Some of its most important battles were fought by school students.

After the Supreme Court announced its decision in *Brown v. Board of Education* in 1954, the court said integration should take place with "all deliberate speed." What does that mean? The southern states decided that it meant with the speed of a snail. So, in the Deep South in 1957, there were still no classrooms where black boys and girls and white boys and girls sat together. Then a federal judge ordered schools in Little Rock, Arkansas, integrated.

Little Rock's Central High School was built in 1928. Some people, then, called it the finest public high school in the nation. Twenty-nine years later, it was still a good school. It had generous playing fields, modern facilities, and more than 2,000 students. But not one black child had ever gone to Central High. In Arkansas, as in all the southern states, laws said that blacks could not go to public schools with whites.

Melba Pattillo wanted to go to Central High. "They had more equipment, they had five floors of opportunities. I understood edu-

You just realize that survival is day to day and you start to grasp the depth of the human spirit, and you start to understand your own ability to cope no matter what. That is the greatest lesson I ever learned.
—MELBA PATTILLO

1957 was the year Dr. Seuss published *The Cat In The Hat*, Althea Gibson became the first black athlete to win a tennis championship at Wimbledon, Smith Corona introduced a portable electric typewriter, teenage girls were wearing poodle skirts and teased hair, Dick Clark helped make rock 'n' roll respectable on TV, and nine black students integrated Little Rock High School.

Nine Brave Kids

In 1987, 30 years after they entered Central High, the Little Rock Nine came together for a reunion. Elizabeth Eckford, now a social worker, was the only one who had stayed in Little Rock. Thelma Mothershed was a teacher in Illinois, Terry Roberts a professor at UCLA, Minnijean Brown a writer and mother of six, Jeff Thomas a Defense Department accountant in California, Ernie Green a vice president of a New York investment firm, Carlotta Walls a Denver realtor, Gloria Ray a magazine publisher living in the Netherlands, and Melba Pattillo a communications consultant and author living in San Francisco. Do you think they might have been strengthened by their struggle? The *Chicago Defender* said: "The Supreme Court ruling would have been meaningless had these Negro boys and girls failed to follow the course mapped out for them by the law....They should be applauded by all of us."

The Little Rock Nine pose with Daisy Bates, president of the Arkansas chapter of the NAACP, during their high school years.

cation before I understood anything else. From the time I was two, my mother said, 'You will go to college. Education is your key to survival,' and I understood that." Otherwise, Melba said, she had no "overwhelming desire to go to this school and integrate this school and change history."

But 15-year-old Melba would change history. She was one of nine black children to integrate Central High. At first, she didn't expect problems. Neither did most other people. Little Rock's citizens thought their city had good race relations. But some people in Little Rock decided to fight integration. They used threats, rocks, and nasty words.

Others, who might have shown some courage, kept quiet. Arkansas's governor, Orval Faubus, announced that he would call in the National Guard. Most people thought the guardsmen would protect the black students, but Faubus meant to use them to keep the nine out of Central High. He knew that aiding integration would make him lose white votes. (And blacks weren't able to vote, so they didn't matter to him.)

Later, Melba remembered:

The first day I was able to enter Central High School, what I felt inside was terrible, wrenching, awful fear. On the car radio I could hear that there was a mob. I knew what a mob meant and I

When Melba Pattillo got to her English class on her first day of school, "One boy jumped up to his feet and began to talk. He told the others to walk out with him because a 'nigger' was in their class. The teacher told him to leave the room." Melba went on, "The boy started for the door and shouted: 'Who's going with me?' No one did. So he said in disgust, 'Chicken!' and left. I had a real nice day."

Figure 1.2 Admit Slip: Civil Rights

chapter, its use increases the probability that students will be prepared for class the following day.

Book Pass

If you want to engage your students by using multiple texts to build background prior to beginning a major unit of study, a Book Pass (Carter and Rashkis 1980) is an effective instructional strategy. This activity is designed to give students the opportunity to briefly examine several books related to a historical time period, an event, or a historical figure. The more diverse the texts in the Book Pass are, the more substantive background students will gain. Using poetry, nonfiction, narrative, informational texts, drama, diaries, primary sources, and art representing the unit to be studied provides them with multiple perspectives.

Depending on your resources and how many encounters with books you would like your students to have, you can arrange Book Passes for groups of students or for the entire class. Whether working with small groups or with the entire class, the procedure for doing a Book Pass is the same.

- Give each student a Book Pass form (see Appendix A).
- Distribute baskets of books if working with small groups or one book to each student if working with the entire class.
- Ask students to note the title and author of a book.
- Then, ask students to sample the book by examining the title and introductions, reading the first few pages, looking at the illustrations, and noting chapter titles/captions/headings.
- As students read, they should note in the comment column at least one new thing they have learned, a connection they have made, or a question they have related to the book's topic.
- After 2–5 minutes, say "book pass" and each student passes his/her book to another student, following the same procedure with the new book.
- At the end of the time you allot for the Book Pass, students can combine the information they have discovered and their questions and connections on a class chart. This information can then guide the study.

In the three samples in Figure 1.3, we can see the range of background knowledge Christine's students have accessed and built with this activity. While two students focused on facts, the third student developed lists of questions that were significant for her after sampling six books. With the sig-

title	comment
Upon the head	no place was safe for Jews with Hitler in power
We remeber the holocaust	they had to live in ghettos, and concentration camps
After the war	Jews tried crossing the ocean to America so they'd survive
I was there.	There was a hitler youth movement
Night	Jews were strangled and killed.
The power of one	Hatred of a similar kind took place in South Africa
I am a star	The auerbachers defied death. for three years and were freed in 1945

Title	Comments
Kinderlager	The Nazis wouldrun about shooting all jews out
A Place to hide	at the end of the Holocaust 6,000,000 jews were killed.
Until we meet again	Polish Cathtolics helped Jews
when the soldiers were gone	The boy lived in Holland
Kris's war	The Nazi's took over Danmark ✳
To Life	russions wento liberate Grafenach
Hanna 3 wolter	The Nazi's forced people to flee the country ✳

Book Pass

title	comments
A pocket full of seeds.	Did the germans only go after the Jews?
Memories of Ann Frank ✳	How did they kill most people.
four Perfect Pebbles	Did Many Jews survive
Kinderlager ✳	How many kids survived Auschwitz - Birkenau?
A place to hide ✳	How old was Ann Frank when killed?
Untill We meet again.	What did they make you do in concentration camps befor you were killed
when the soilders went gone.	What did the soilders do to the kids?

Figure 1.3 Book Passes

nificant amount of information they now have, Christine can now help the students organize and synthesize prior to reading the related chapters in their textbooks. Having encountered content-specific language, dates, historical figures, facts, and emotional content, these students are ready to read their textbooks and do research.

Here and Now

A Here and Now (Kirby, Liner and Vinz 1988) is a form of academic writing that students do to activate background and anticipate the content for a day's lesson. It is a "quick write," which can be based on a prompt or visual. Anticipating content is a critical stage of lesson planning, as it is during this time that students are exposed to rich content from which they are able to make connections and ask questions. Part of making connections occurs as we think through our background in order to anticipate learning something new we can connect to that background. Unlike a typical writing prompt where students respond in order to develop fluency, a Here and Now is connected to the content to be explored that day.

Prior to reading "War and the Scientists" in *A History of US, Book 10*, Christine showed her students a picture of an atom bomb's mushroom cloud. She used a Here and Now to help them focus the questions the picture raised for them. Kari's response indicates the impact of these encounters with the content:

> At first I thought Pearl Harbor was big "woop." But when I saw that clip it sent chills down my spine—made me go white. I just didn't believe what I was seeing. Why did that have to happen?

Berthie was also changed by these encounters:

> I thought it was quite scary. I personally think I couldn't make it through something that dangerous. I think whoever was there at the time and is still living could go through any kind of fear. This is something someone just can't forget. Watching all that bombing and killing makes me wonder what would I do if I was in such a situation. I wonder how the people flying that plane felt afterwards. I also wondered if after the war was over if the person who sent them to war felt bad about how many innocent people died?

As we think about the relatively short amount of time it takes to help students build background knowledge that is meaningful and memorable and triggers such thoughtful questions, we can see the value in asking students to do a quick Here and Now to compose their thoughts prior to reading.

Skimming and Scanning

Teaching struggling readers how to Skim and Scan is a very painful process. In fact, most students believe that all words in the text are equally important or equally unimportant. Skimming and Scanning require that readers use their knowledge of ways to get information from text quickly. Students have to learn where in the text they would go to get first impressions and fast facts related to the reading they will do. Then, they have to make some predictions and inferences based on those impressions and facts.

The example in Figure 1.4 represents students learning how to Skim and Scan as a way to build background knowledge, make predictions and inferences of content, and generate questions they would still want to answer. In this case, students are using *A History of US, Book 10*, reading chapter 31. As a way to teach students how to Skim and Scan, we have used a graphic organizer (see Figure 1.4) to help them organize their thoughts by looking at three processes: acquiring first impressions, gathering information, and, using those first impressions and fast facts to generate some final thoughts prior to reading.

Christine's students have learned several basic aspects of how to Skim and Scan while also building background knowledge:

- Use the title to activate/build background knowledge
- Look at the pictures and the people in the pictures
- Look at maps/timelines/graphs/charts
- Look at glossary words
- Read information in fact boxes
- Read information in sidebars
- Read captions
- Read first and last paragraphs
- Read highlighted information or bold words

In Figure 1.4, one student's graphic shows that she has used the information she gained from these categories to generate some questions, make predictions, and use highlighted words to connect to what she infers is the important context. In this way, two broad goals have been achieved: she now has background knowledge to take into her reading, and research, and she has access to information that tells her whether or not this is a viable source for the work she has to do.

Skimming & Scanning

First Impressions	Fast Facts	"Final Thoughts"
		Ask myself questions
* Read title: "Picking and Picketing"	* Read the poem by Gomez-Peña	* Why did Chávez stop eating?
* Look at sad faces.		
* Look at pictures * Look at last sentence "Cesar Chávez started eating again"	* Read the captions under the pictures.	* I think this chapter is going to tell us how hard migrant workers' lives are.
* Look at map pg. 156	* Read the introduction/first few sentences.	* One of the important words was coffin—someone must have died?
* Look at words in yellow boxes and information in purple boxes 	* Read highlighted information in sidebars * Read the last paragraph. 	* It said picketing in the title. Workers must have been angry. 

©Janet Allen

Figure 1.4

Writing to Learn

In my classroom, I often tried using a K-W-L approach (Ogle 1986) at the beginning of a unit or the study of a historical event. I usually met with an amazing lack of success. I would ask my students what they knew (K) about a topic and they would say, "Nothing." When I asked them what they wanted to know (W), they would say, "Nothing." I finally realized that a K-W-L was going to work with my students only if I did something to build background and create an emotional connection to the topic we were going to study. The night after the "Silver War" debacle in my classroom, I created Writing to Learn (Allen and Gonzalez 1998; Allen 2000) as a way to help my students develop meaningful connections to historical events.

Writing to Learn offers students a variety of experiences with several texts. In the Writing to Learn form used here (Figure 1.5), Rosangel has responded to Christine's reading of information from three different sources. However, you could choose as many sources as it takes to meet the two purposes of Writing to Learn: providing students with rich context and emotional impact for an event or topic. In this case, she has chosen two excerpts from a textbook plus a picture book, *The Number on My Grandfather's Arm* (Adler, David 1987), to introduce students to the Holocaust. The sources you choose could be fiction, nonfiction, poetry, news articles, video, news clips, periodicals, artifacts, interviews, art, or music. Teacher Kyle Gonzalez (Allen and Gonzalez 1998) even used a speaker for one of the sources. As you choose and order the sources you will use, the critical aspect is that each new experience builds on the previous one by adding more information and/or emotional content.

Christine chose as her first source the glossary definition of "Holocaust" from one of her textbooks, *The American Journey* (Applebee 1998), because she wanted her students to have a working definition for the term before encountering it in other contexts. The textbook defined the "Holocaust" as "the name given to the mass slaughter of Jews and other groups by the Nazis during World War II." Students read the definition and then wrote a response to what they just read (see Figure 1.5, column 1).

For column 2, Christine chose to use the textbook again, this time reading five paragraphs (758–759) and studying the photograph that accompanied those paragraphs. The reading distilled the events into its basics: Hitler, the final solution, the concentration camps, Auschwitz, and two quotes from the time. As short as it was, this reading still had the power to silence the students with the magnitude of the event. In spite of its brevity, it gave students

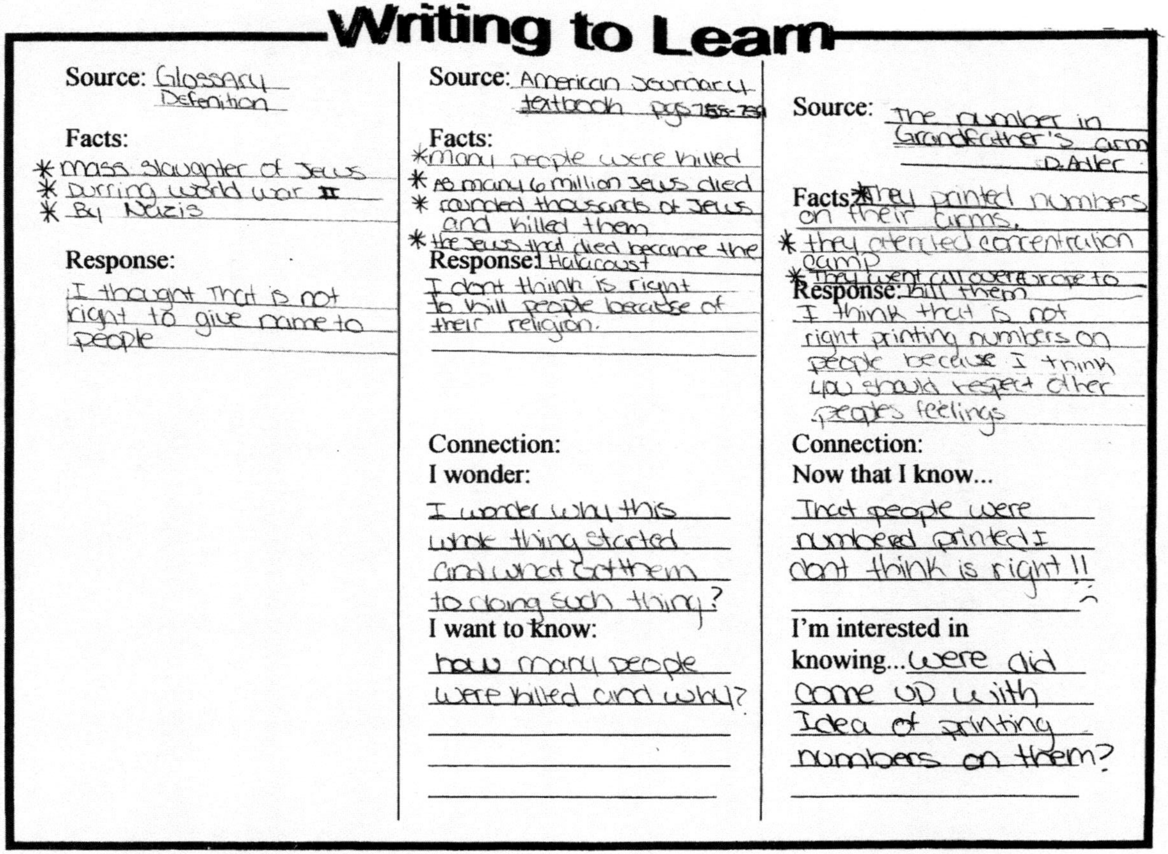

Writing to Learn

Source: Glossary Definition

Facts:
* Mass slaughter of Jews
* During world war II
* By Nazis

Response:
* I thought that is not right to give harm to people

Source: American Secondary textbook Pg 155-159

Facts:
* Many people were killed
* 6 million to 7 million Jews died
* caused thousands of Jews and killed them
* he suschied died because the

Response: Holocaust
* I don think is right to kill people because of their religion.

Connection:
I wonder:
I wonder why this whole thing started and what happen to along such thing?

I want to know:
how many people were killed and why?

Source: The number in Grandfather's arm –Adler

Facts: They printed numbers on their arms.
* they crimied concentration camp
* They sent all people arose to them.

Response:
I think that is not right printing numbers on people because I think you should respect other people's feelings

Connection:
Now that I know...
That people were numbered printed. I don think is right !!

I'm interested in knowing... were did came up with idea of printing numbers on them?

Figure 1.5 Writing to Learn: Holocaust

enough information for questions for their "I wonder" and "I want to know" sentence completions (column 2).

Finally, she read Adler's picture book, *The Number on My Grandfather's Arm.* The book uses actual black-and-white photographs of a grandfather and his granddaughter in their apartment building as the grandfather explains why a number is tattooed on his arm. The man in the pictures is a Holocaust survivor, and the content is a powerful reading and writing experience for students.

In using Writing to Learn as a way to make history meaningful and memorable, Christine built on the reciprocal nature and value of reading and writing in content classes. "The more content is manipulated, the more likely it is understood and remembered. In accordance with this thesis, a number of researchers have hypothesized that writing will have an impact upon what is learned because it prompts learners to elaborate and manipulate ideas" (Tierney and Shanahan 1991, 266). Writing to Learn offers students the opportunity to view an event from several angles, inviting them to record information and respond to what they have learned by making connections and asking questions. Most students leave Writing to Learn wanting to know more, which is always a goal for us in reading history.

Anticipating Content Language

Word study can be an important vehicle for building background and anticipating content. While word study can be done at any time in your history class, it is best to teach words at, or close to, the point of need. In the next chapter, I address word study as a way to support and monitor comprehension, but in this chapter I want to address using word study as a way for you to assess students' background knowledge, to build on the background knowledge they bring, and to anticipate content.

As we look for ways to use words as a pre-reading support, one of the instructional strategies we shouldn't overlook is the value of rich read-alouds and shared reading. It was interesting to me to read a *Time* magazine article (Wallis 1998) in which the writer quotes the director of admissions at Williams College, who cited the impact of rich reading lives on SAT scores. "Parker says he has never met a kid with high scores on the verbal section of the SAT who wasn't a passionate reader."

The admissions director's statement is consistent with the existing research that the amount of reading is the best predictor of vocabulary growth (Fielding, Wilson, and Anderson, 1986). In fact, as William Nagy states, "What is needed to produce vocabulary growth is not more vocabulary instruction, but more reading" (1988). Teachers who read a wide variety of historical texts to their students find that the reading builds background for the content they are studying, creates engaged and interested learners, and helps students develop rich word banks for content reading and reading.

Christine reads aloud to the students in her history class every day. Some days she does a read-aloud while students do not have the text in front of them. At such times, they are listening to the text and gaining content knowledge from the text choices she has made. At other times, she does a shared reading, when all of the students have a copy of the text and can follow along. During these times, students can revisit the text and gather words related to the historical time periods, events, or documents. They are able to categorize these words as *high-utility* words, words that are so common in reading and writing history, that students will want to learn these words for other reading. These high-utility words are then added to the word wall (see photograph in Figure 1.6). The word wall shown in Figure 1.6 is organized alpha-

Figure 1.6   Word Wall

betically so that students will be able to access historical language quickly for use in their writing. Words can be changed on the word wall, depending on how you choose to use the wall. For example, Christine often asks students to revisit the word wall at the beginning of a unit to see if there are words they would want to remove and new words they would add that would help them in their study of the current unit.

At an early stage of each unit, Christine provides students with a Things We Can Read graphic organizer (see Appendix A for master). Students can then keep personal word walls, where they record language related to their reading and writing. Figure 1.7 shows one student's personal word wall for the Hispanic American study the class did. Christine takes a few moments after shared reading each day for students to gather content-specific words they want to save. Their topical lists are connected to a specific historical event or time period being studied.

Word study activities often precede the actual unit as a way for students to anticipate the content of the unit. Christine uses the word study to assess students' current background for the study they will begin together and to build students' knowledge where none may have existed. In this section, I will highlight three strategies that we have found particularly useful for assessment and building of background: List-Group-Label, Predict-O-Gram, and Story Impressions.

List-Group-Label

Finding out what students know about a concept or event is critical to our understanding of how we will craft instruction to overcome students' lack of background knowledge or how we will build on what they know to add to their current understanding. List-Group-Label (Taba 1967) is a brainstorming activity that can serve a variety of instructional purposes. Observing students in the process of the activity can help us assess their basic understanding of a concept. As students group their words, we can see whether they have a surface knowledge of the word or concept or an in-depth understanding. Finally, having students listen to the words their peers generate helps build word and concept knowledge for all members of the group.

When using List-Group-Label with her students, Christine modeled the activity by asking them to brainstorm words they thought of when she said the word, "war." They wrote for one minute, and then she asked each student for one word. She recorded these words on an overhead transparency and then asked the students to figure out four possible categories into which they

Hispanic american

Things We Can Read...

ABC	DEF	GHI	JKL
Brazil coffee Costa Rica Cuba Christopher Columbus Colombia caribean Chile Argentina cathedral Beaches	Dominican Republic Fidel Castro empanadas	Hispanic Immigrant Haiti Indians	Jamaica Juan Ponce De Leon Latin
MNO	PQR	STU	VWX
Mexico/mexican mariachi band mango	Puerto Rico (rich port) Peru Plantain plumeria Plantain	Trujillo Spanish uruguai tostones Spain Santo Domingo Tampa salsa Sugar canes money Taino Bacardi Simon Bolivar	Venezuela
YZ			

©Janet Allen 2000

Figure 1.7 Personal Word Wall

List - group - label: War

death	blood
attack	
A bombs.	
A Guns	
fight	
Army	
A muskets	
revolution	
D family	
D Idependence	
B frustration	
D racism	
C 9/11	
B victory	
A helicopters	
B bad words	
B sadness	
people dying	
D disagreement	
B courageous	
hospitals	
B madness	
B aggression	
C my country	
A fire	
pain	
D revenge	

Figure 1.8   Group Word List

could sort their words. Students worked with partners to sort the words into categories. When they finished, she asked them to explain why they chose to put words in specific categories. For example, one student chose to put the word "people" into a category titled "Transportation." He defended his decision; because people use transportation to get to and from wars, he thought the two went together during wartime. As students are engaged in this activity, they are activating the background they bring to the topic, using that background to support their opinions and making connections to new information they gain from their peers.

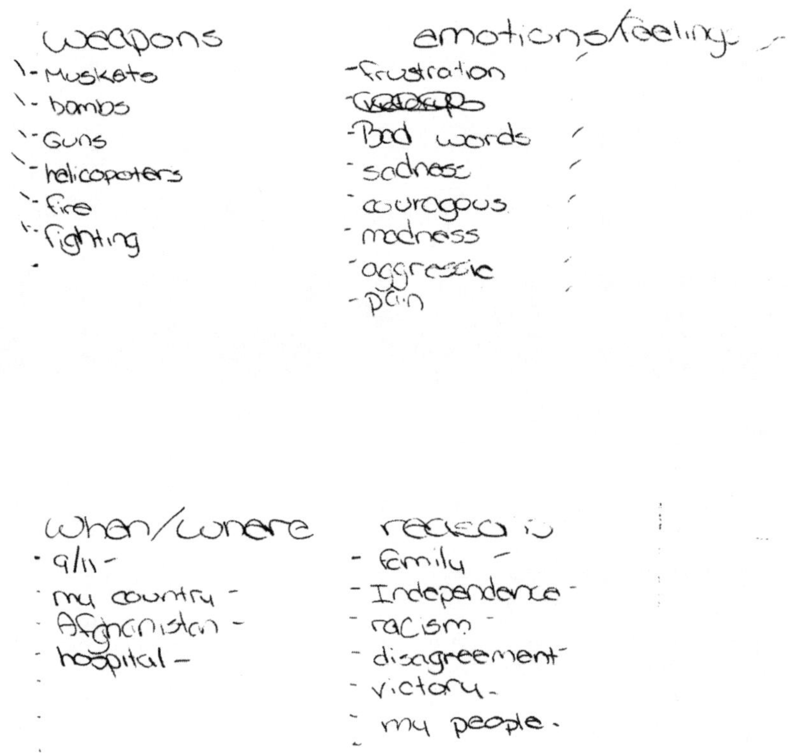

Weapons
- Muskets
- bombs
- Guns
- helicopters
- fire
- fighting

emotions/feeling
- frustration
- ~~anger~~
- Bad words
- sadness
- couragous
- madness
- aggressive
- pain

when/where
- 9/11
- my country
- Afghanistan
- hospital

reasons
- family
- Independence
- racism
- disagreement
- victory
- my people

Figure 1.9 Words Listed by Categories

After the activity is modeled for students, they can work in small groups to do List-Group-Label, using the following steps:

1. Give students a concept or word and ask them to brainstorm as many words related to the concept word as they can think of. I always give students a minimum number, such as seven words.
2. Ask students to combine their individual lists with the lists of other students in their group. Figure 1.8 represents the words generated by members of one group.
3. Students are then asked to take the list representing all the words from their group members and categorize the words in a way that makes sense in relation to the concept word they were given. In Figure 1.9, these students have grouped their words into four groups and labeled them in the categories of weapons related to war, emotions/feelings connected to war, reasons for having war, and when/where wars are fought.

Once students have had the opportunity to discuss the words and contribute their words and categories to those of the entire class, words can be chosen from all the lists to add to a unit word wall supporting the current study.

Predict-O-Gram

A Predict-O-Gram (Blachowicz 1986) is a set of words taken from a text you are planning to read with your students or assign for independent reading. Students are given a list of words and asked to use their background knowledge and knowledge of the text to predict how those words might be used in subsequent reading. I find a Predict-O-Gram works best when we read a portion of the text to students and then give them a list of words that occur in the text after we stop reading. In this way, students have some common knowledge from the shared reading to combine with their background knowledge when making predictions from the list of words.

In the example highlighted here, the teacher has read the first page and a half of chapter 19 from *A History of US, Book 10,* "Some Brave Children Meet a Roaring Bull." Reading the beginning of the chapter aloud to students as they follow along gives these students a context for the events highlighted in this chapter. The teacher stopped reading when Martin Luther King, Jr., was introduced into the text. She then gave students the following words and asked them to use the words to predict the remaining content of the chapter.

Dramatic	Organize	Demonstrators	Courage
Respect	Civil Rights	Leader	Birmingham
Marches	Movement	Overcome	Fear
Dogs	Sit-ins	Boycott	Alabama

Students used the word list to connect the words to the reading they had just heard, to make predictions, and to form questions they hoped the remaining text would answer.

Story Impressions

The instructional activity Story Impressions (McGinley and Denner 1987) also helps students build background knowledge and supports them in using that knowledge to anticipate content. Students are presented with a list of words in a vertical format. Students then work in small groups to add words to the word list to complete sentences that would make sense given the context provided (historical event, biography, time period, historical novel, and the like). The following example was created using the book jacket of Kathryn Lasky's historical novel *Beyond the Burning Time*. The novel is set during the Salem witch trials. In order to create the Story Impression, I have simply eliminated some of the words from the jacket description so that students can create sentences by adding words they think fit. The list of words includes some, but not all, of the words on the book jacket. The words listed are in the order they appear on the jacket.

Beyond the Burning Time, Kathryn Lasky

year	God-fearing	begin
1691	Salem	brutal
darkness	really	shocking
houses	witches	history
Village	spells	Kathryn Lasky
Twelve	Mary's	dramatic
Mary Chase	As	story
filled	Mary	about
fear	mother	good
several	struggle	and
begun	farm	our
strange	event	spower
Can	not only	choices
true	peace	
some	village	
respectable	but also	

Students should be able to fill in enough words to make the text meaningful by reading each column from top to bottom inserting words to make complete sentences. When this occurs, these words and sentences can then be used to construct context for the novel. In so doing, we create a bridge between the teacher's purposes for text selection and students developing their own purposes for reading. One example of a completed Story Impression for this text follows:

Beyond the Burning Time, Kathryn Lasky

The **year** is	**God-fearing** people	**begin** to get
1691 and a	in **Salem** are	**brutal**
darkness has settled	**really**	This **shocking**
over the **houses** in	**witches** casting	**history**, retold by
the **Village.**	**spells?**	**Kathryn Lasky**, is the
Twelve year old	**Mary's** life begins	**dramatic**
Mary Chase is	to change **As**	**story**
filled with	**Mary** and her	**about**
fear.	**mother**	**good** vs. evil
There are **several**	**struggle** to work	**and** how
People who have **begun**	the **farm**	**our**
acting **strange**	**events**	**power** comes from
Can it be	**not only** rob them	our **choices.**
true that	of the **peace**	
some of the	of their **village**	
respectable	**but also**	

This is the example of a completed Story Impression. Bold words are those inserted by students as words that would make sense to them as a predictor of content.

Developing a Purpose for Reading

When we provide experiences that ask readers to develop their own questions prior to reading a text, we address several goals: we have given them the opportunity to think about the topic, to synthesize their understandings, to connect new information to those understandings, and to generate questions that will make their study more meaningful. All of these cognitive tasks help readers establish purposes for reading. When they do, they have moved from a passive reader stance to active reading. We have used many instructional strategies to support students in establishing a purpose for reading. Some, like the K-W-L (Ogle 1986) and K-W-L Plus (Carr and Ogle 1987), are mainstays in many history classrooms. We have chosen to highlight two additional strategies that prompt critical thinking and invite students to read: Anticipation Guide and Concept Ladder.

Anticipation Guide

An Anticipation Guide (Readence, Bean, and Baldwin 1985) is a prereading guide that asks students to confront critical issues, value statements, and information related to reading the teacher plans to do. The guides serve as a connection between students' background, their beliefs and ideas, and those concepts and ideas they will encounter in their study. Guides are created by the teacher and can be used as the basis for both pre- and post-reading. You can quickly create an anticipation guide using the following steps:

- Select the theme or topic for your next unit of study.
- Identify some critical ideas, information, or issues that will arise in the course of the study.
- Highlight the ideas or issues for which students may hold background knowledge or have opinions.
- Write statements (3–8) that will foster discussion around the ideas and issues. Statements should be ones to which students can respond without having read the text. These are not comprehension questions; rather, they are opinion/belief statements.
- Ask students to read each statement and then to write whether they agree or disagree with the statement.
- Provide a space for students to write comments that support their opinions.
- Read the text (or assign the text for independent or group reading) and then have students revisit each statement. At this point, they are determining whether they agree or disagree with the statement after the reading. Again, they can comment on why their opinions have remained the same or have changed as a result of the reading.
- Use students' responses to the guide as the basis for class discussion, further reading, and research.

The following anticipation guide was constructed by Christine prior to a study of the U.S. internment camps for Japanese and Japanese-Americans during World War II. As part of this unit, students will read Graham Salisbury's novel, *Under the Blood-Red Sun.*

Anticipation Guide: *Under the Blood-Red Sun,* Graham Salisbury

1. The United States government has a right to make us give up our homes if it decides it is good for the country.

   Agree   Disagree   Comments:

2. The United States has done some bad things, but at least it has never done anything so bad as the concentration camps during the Holocaust.

Agree   Disagree   Comments:

3. If you come from another country, you should be more loyal to that country than to the country to which you have moved.

Agree   Disagree   Comments:

4. People are more loyal to their country than to their race.

Agree   Disagree   Comments:

5. In a time of war, the safety of a country is more important than personal civil rights.

Agree   Disagree   Comments:

After individual students complete the anticipation guide and after student groups have had the opportunity to meet and discuss their comments, students then journal about their rationales for their positions. This activity can take place as students are introduced to the event or concept and can be revisited throughout the unit.

Concept Ladder

A Concept Ladder (Gillet and Temple 1982) is an advance organizer that helps students organize and synthesize their understandings of a topic or event in order to articulate questions around the topic/event. After the teacher builds some background knowledge with students by using art, music, shared texts, video, or presentation, students are asked to create a concept ladder that will provide questions to guide their reading and research. A question is noted on each rung of the ladder. Students can keep individual concept ladders and find answers to their own questions, or you can construct a concept ladder with the entire group and use those questions as part of the basis for your unit study.

Students enjoy creating these concept ladders and searching for answers to the questions they have generated. Before her students created the questions in the graphic organizer in Figure 1.10, Christine showed them a video clip and read a brief excerpt about the atomic bomb. After these two experiences, her students generated the following questions for their group concept ladder:

- Why did the United States drop the bomb on Japan?
- Who started World War II?

- Why was the bomb built?
- How many people did it kill?
- Who made the decision to drop it?
- How long does radiation last?
- How did radiation affect unborn children?
- How big was the bomb?
- How high was the mushroom cloud?
- How does an atomic bomb work?
- How long did it take to build?
- Why was it dropped on Hiroshima and Nagasaki?
- How long did the war last?

As you can see from the concept ladders in Figure 1.10, students were able to answer some of their questions by reading their textbooks and the supplemental sources Christine made available to them. The two concept ladders shown in Figure 1.10 demonstrate that there was some overlap in questions between groups, with all groups asking similar questions, but each group also generated some questions unique to its discussion. Questions that were unanswered on the group concept ladders formed the rungs on the class concept ladder. These questions were then revisited during the course of the unit.

The time you allocate for assessing and building background knowledge with your students will pay huge dividends as students read their textbooks and embark on research. Activities done during this stage of learning will lead to higher levels of student interest and engagement, support critical thinking, help students make connections and discover patterns, and acquire language that will support their reading and writing in history. In Zemelman, Daniels and Hyde's *Best Practice: New Standards for Teaching and Learning in America's Schools*, the authors make this statement: "Social studies are about phenomena to be explored, not just answers to memorize" (1998, 143). Planning for time to build background knowledge in meaningful and memorable ways helps students want to begin the exploration. When students *want* to learn, half the battle is won.

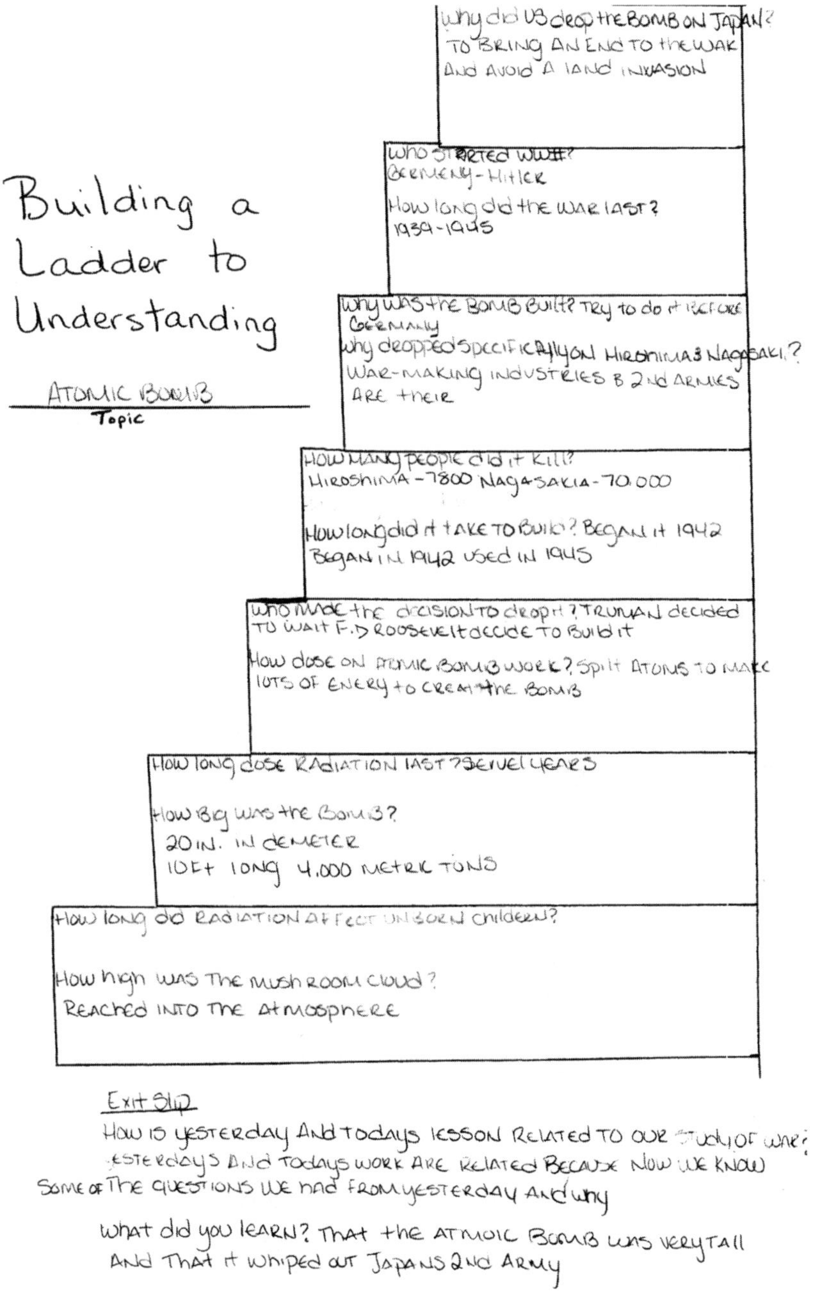

Building a
Ladder to
Understanding

ATOMIC BOMB
Topic

Why did US drop the BOMB ON JAPAN?
TO BRING AN END to the WAR
And Avoid A land invasion

Who Started WWII?
GERMANY - Hitler

How long did the WAR lAST?
1939-1945

Why WAS the BOMB Built? TRy to do it BEFORE
GERMANY
Why dropped SPECIFICALLY ON Hiroshima & Nagasaki?
WAR-MAKING INDUSTRIES B 2Nd ARMIES
ARE their

HOW MANY PEOPLE did it kill?
Hiroshima - 7800 Nagasakia - 70.000

How long did it tAKE TO BUILD? BEgAN it 1942
BEgAN IN 1942 USED IN 1945

Who MADE the decision TO drop it? TRUMAN decided
TO WAIT F.D ROOSEVEIt decide TO Build it

How dose ON ATOMIC BOMB WORK? SPliT ATOMS TO MAKE
loTS OF ENERY to CREATE the BOMB

How long dose RADIATION lAST? SERVEL YEARS

How Big WAS the BOMB?
20 IN. IN dEMETER
10 Ft lONg 4,000 METRIC TONS

How long did RADIATION AFFECT UN BORN Children?

How high WAS THE MUSH ROOM Cloud?
REACHED INTO THE Atmosphere

Exit Slip
How is yesterday And todays lesson RelAted TO OUR Study OF WAR?
Yesterdays And todays work Are RelATed BECAUSE NOW WE KNOW
SOME OF THE questions WE HAd FROM yesterday And why

What did you lEARN? That the ATMOIC BOMB WAS VERY TAll
And THAT it whiped out JAPANS 2Nd ARMy

Figure 1.10a Concept Ladder

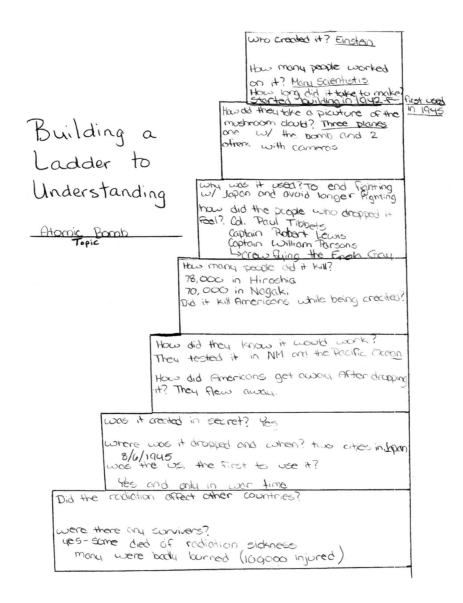

Building a
Ladder to
Understanding

Atomic Bomb
Topic

Who created it? Einstein

How many people worked
on it? Many scientists
How long did it take to make?
started building in 1942 - First used
in 1945
How did they take a picture of the
mushroom cloud? Three planes
one w/ the bomb and 2
others with cameras

why was it used? To end fighting
w/ Japan and avoid longer fighting

how did the people who dropped it
feel? Col. Paul Tibbets
Captain Robert Lewis
Captain William Parsons
↳ crew flying the Enola Gay

How many people did it kill?
78,000 in Hiroshia
70,000 in Nagaki
Did it kill Americans while being created?

How did they know it would work?
They tested it in NM and the Pacific Ocean

How did Americans get away After dropping
it? They flew away.

was it created in secret? Yes

Where was it dropped and when? two cities in Japan
8/6/1945
was the US. the first to use it?

Yes and only in war time

Did the radiation affect other countries?

were there any survivers?
yes - some died of radiation sickness
many were badly burned (10go000 injured)

Figure 1.10b Concept Ladder *(continued)*

Chapter 2

Providing Ongoing Support
Supporting and Monitoring Comprehension during Reading

"As teachers, we cannot simply define what our students already do well or what we like to teach. We need to have a clear sense of the range of strategies all readers should have at their disposal, and to insure that our students develop these."

Blachowicz and Ogle (2001, 13)

When adults talk about reading history, most of us think of a range of history-related texts: historical fiction, periodicals, biographies, diaries, documents, reports, and documentaries. Yet, when I talk with students about reading history, they immediately talk about reading history textbooks. This leads me to believe that our task as teachers is twofold: expanding the range of reading that students define as reading history and increasing students' ability to comprehend that range of texts—including their textbooks. Much of the comprehension support we provide during reading is focused on helping students negotiate a range of texts.

For many students, obstacles to comprehension occur when they are presented with a diverse range of text types. Several aspects are involved in supporting students' comprehension in reading history, because comprehension is always a complex issue. Nagy highlights the complexity of comprehension with this statement in *Teaching Vocabulary to Improve Reading Comprehension*: "Reading comprehension depends on a wealth of encyclopedic knowledge and not merely on definitional knowledge of the words in the text" (1988, 7). While lists of vocabulary words are often introduced to students prior to assigning reading, it is clear that comprehending reading assignments is about more than defining words.

In order for students to comprehend the diverse types of texts they encounter in reading history, they must know how to use and when to employ a wide range of independent reading strategies. Those challenges to comprehension include, but are not limited to, the following text-related reading issues:

- Diverse levels of readability are represented in a single text.
- Texts present multiple concepts in a short amount of space (concept density).
- Knowledge on how to use text supports to support reading is lacking.
- Ability to break the language code (specialized vocabulary) is required.
- Comprehension is predicated on significant background knowledge.
- Sophisticated study/memory techniques have to be employed to organize and retain information.
- Monitoring techniques have to be employed so important concepts aren't missed.
- Knowledge of what supplemental resources (atlas, map, almanac) can provide is necessary.
- Knowledge of how to read supplemental resources is required.
- Texts may not hold or capture reader's interest so readers must be self-motivated.
- Multiple texts must be held in memory for comparison, contrast, and discovery of patterns.
- Ability to determine which information is critical and which is secondary is needed.
- Knowledge of how to determine bias, author's motivation, and subtext is required.
- Ability to differentiate fact from opinion is necessary.
- Ability to negotiate a variety of text structures is necessary.
- Assessment/evaluation often requires high levels of both literal and inferential comprehension.

Can a process this complex really be taught?

Research provides strong support for the belief that comprehension can be taught. In 1985, Anderson and colleagues, the authors of *Becoming a Nation of Readers*, cited the importance of instruction in reading strategies:

"Teacher-led instruction in reading strategies and other aspects of comprehension promotes reading achievement, but there is very little direct comprehension instruction in most American classrooms" (118). Fortunately, this pattern has been changing in the last decade. Many teachers demonstrate comprehension strategies on a daily basis to and with their students, providing them with opportunities for guided and independent practice to implement the strategies.

This direct instruction in comprehension strategies is critical in content classes because it helps students understand how to focus their reading. In a chapter in Taylor, Graves, and van den Broek's text, *Reading for Meaning: Fostering Comprehension in the Middle Grades*, van den Broek and Kremer highlight the criticality of this issue: "Successful comprehension depends in part on readers' ability to allocate their limited attention efficiently and effectively to the most relevant pieces of information within the text and within their memory" (2000, 7). Thus, the best place for students to learn how to comprehend a variety of history texts is within the context of real reading for real purposes.

The question in many schools is not whether comprehension can be taught, but who should teach it. The authors of *Becoming a Nation of Readers* address that issue as well: "The most logical place for instruction in most reading and thinking strategies is in social studies and science rather than in separate lessons about reading. The reason is that the strategies are useful mainly when the student is grappling with important but unfamiliar content" (Anderson et al. 1985, 73). If we want students to read history with confidence and competence, then we have to take on the task of teaching them how to read history and historical texts. The positive aspects of sharing diverse texts with students is realized only when we have ensured that students can read those texts independently.

Freebody and Luke (1990, 7–16) have determined four broad roles for readers that will help them read independently: Meaning Maker, Code Breaker, Text User, and Text Critic. Each of these roles contributes to successful comprehension, and each can be taught and reinforced through direct instruction and demonstrations by the teacher and guided practice and independent use by the students. As we now look at strategies for supporting and monitoring students' comprehension, we organize the strategies according to Freebody and Luke's roles for readers. In this chapter, we focus on the first three (Meaning Maker, Code Breaker and Text User) as aspects of supporting and monitoring comprehension. The role of Text Critic will be used to frame the strategies in Chapter 3.

Meaning Maker:
Conversation, Connections, and Commitment

In Allington and Johnston's research study, reported in *Reading to Learn* (2002), the authors cite the role of classroom conversation as one of the most critical factors in supporting comprehension.

> The talk in these classrooms was also connective. That is, these teachers routinely connected (1) topics under study to earlier topics and to students' experiences and background knowledge, (2) authors to other works by the same author and to other authors' works, (3) strategies from one subject to another, (4) lessons from one week or month to the next, and so on. When the teachers weren't making such connections explicitly, they were asking students to consider connections. (2002, 207)

When students are reading history, this talk is essential to their understanding. Because most students bring little background knowledge to the reading, classroom conversations help establish and reestablish time frames, context, patterns, and connections.

In this excerpt from Christine's teaching journal, she reflects on the opportunity her student, Natalia, gave her to think about the conversations and connections required to help students make a commitment to reading and learning.

> While some of my students were committed students who loved history and planned to go to college, Natalia just wanted to get out of school and get married. Boys were the main topic of conversation for her and that conversation was usually followed by anything related to makeup, clothing or other girls. She could have been a great student, but her focus was just on other things. On the day we were studying women's lives in the 1700s, learning about their jobs, clothing and lifestyle, Natalia finally found her history connection.
>
> "Ms. Landaker, didn't they make girls wear chastity belts back then?"
>
> "Um, well, I don't know how common they were, but, yes, I believe they may still have been around somewhere. Or, at least, the threat of them still existed. I haven't read much about them."
>
> "So, Ms. L., I have a question. How did girls, well, y'know, when they had their you-know-what?"
>
> At this point, I was hoping the conversation wasn't going where I thought it was; but, alas. . .
>
> "What did they do when they had their periods?" she asked—loudly. Loudly enough for the other five groups to hear. All ears were on us now.

"Um, well, um, I, um. . . I don't know. I guess it would have been a bit inconvenient, but I suppose they were made so that women could relieve themselves without having to be unlocked each time, so I guess they just kind of adjusted. . . Natalia, I just don't know. Where could we look that up?"

It was at this point that I realized just what it would take for students like Natalia to be become connected to history.

James Britton says that "writing floats on a sea of talk" (1970, 164). I would contend that all learning is enhanced and accelerated if we maximize the use of that "sea of talk." The instructional strategies we describe in this section support the conversation and connections that help students make a commitment to learning.

Questions Game

The most effective strategy I have used for getting students to ask important questions of their reading is to use an activity by Frank McTeague called the Questions Game (*Yellow Brick Roads,* Allen 2000, 166–69). Developed by McTeague, this strategy was initially described in Aidan Chambers' book, *Tell Me: Children, Reading, and Talk* (1996, 115) to support connections, deep thinking, and the questioning of texts they read. Steps we take when using the Questions Game follow:

- Each student reads the assigned text and writes down three questions he or she would like answered. (10 minutes)
- Students choose a partner, exchange questions, and try to answer each other's questions. I usually have students try to do this in writing before they share together. (5 minutes)
- Partners then sit together to discuss answers to each other's questions. At the end of the discussion time, these partners form three new questions. These questions can be extensions of questions they had in their original sets, questions that remain unanswered, or new questions that came out of their discussion. (10–15 minutes)
- Each two-person team exchanges questions with another two-person team. The partners discuss the questions they have received and attempt to answer them. (10 minutes)
- The two, two-person teams who have exchanged questions combine into a four-person group. The four readers discuss the six questions represented in their group. (10 minutes)

- When time is called, each four-person group comes up with one question that is still unanswered or that they would like to bring to the whole-class discussion.

This activity can be used multiple times and with any type of text. In this example, Christine has used the questioning activity with her students after they read chapter 26, "A Final Solution," in *War, Peace, and All That Jazz (A History of US, Book 9)*. The student samples of questions shown in Figure 2.1 represent two pairs of students exchanging questions with each other. This activity represents the first two bulleted items from the preceding instructions. At the bottom of each set of questions (Figure 2.1), students have written the post-discussion questions they have generated with their learning partners.

When the two, two-person teams were combined, each four-person group generated one question that was important enough for them to bring to the class discussion. This middle school class generated the following list of those important questions:

- What religion were the non-Jewish kids that weren't allowed in the U.S.?
- Did anyone in Anne Frank's family survive?
- What did the Imperial Wizard of the KKK have to do with what we read?
- Was it true that Hitler was part Jewish?
- What did Hitler have against the non-Jewish kids that were part of the 20,000 he tried to send to America?
- Why were Jews Hitler's main target?
- How many non-Jews died in the camps?
- How many Jews escaped from the Nazis?
- How did Anne Frank get into a killing camp and have her diary published?
- What are Quakers?
- How did the Holocaust finally end?
- How did Hitler die?

The results from Christine's students mirror the results I always get when using this activity. By the end of the activity, students have read the text several times and have refined their questions to represent significant areas of interest and concern to them. These questions then lead to the important talk that makes students more committed to further reading and research.

1. Who is Anne Frank? Anne Franks was a girl and her family hid in an attic and lived their for quite some time and she wrote in a diary of all her days. Some one found out they were hiding and turned them in.

2. What are some ways they'd kill the people? gas chambers, shooting, starvation, and beating.

_____

3. Why did Americans turn the 20,000 children down They were to stupid to think why we came to america and the battles we fought.

*_____ *_____ A

1. How did Anne Frank and her family survive, without leaving the house.
by byeing a lot of food to store

2. Did anybody in her family live? no
Did anybody from Anne Frank's family survive

1). why did Hitler want to kill the children? because he doesn't want Jewish to reproduce.

2) what did the Americans have to do with Hitler

3). what is anti-semitism?

1) what is anti-semitism?
2) why did Hitler feel the way he feel about children under 14?

What did he have against kids under 14 years of age were'nt Jewish?

Figure 2.1   Student Questions (Individual and Combined)

ReQuest

ReQuest (Manzo, 1969) serves as an excellent tool for helping students monitor their comprehension. When students have completed their reading of a text, this activity gives them an enjoyable way to review information, synthesize main ideas, develop higher-level questions, and focus on the most important points from the text. Students can participate in this activity by using the following steps:

- Prior to assigning reading, you should use supplemental resources to build background knowledge and foster engagement. You might show a video clip, read a related poem, connect upcoming reading to their lives, or share your experiences and knowledge of the subject. This will lead to more students participating in the ReQuest activity.
- Give students a reading assignment that relates to the current topic or unit of study. While students are reading, you might want to read and review the text as well and generate several higher-order comprehension questions you will eventually ask of the students. When forming your questions, model higher-order questioning by progressing from literal questions to questions that require reading between the lines, making world connections, and examining influence and motivation.
- Students can work individually or with partners to refine their questions so that they have the best possible questions to ask you.
- As students ask you questions they have developed about the reading, you and the students may need to revisit the text in order to answer those questions that are too challenging or need clarification. Students should also revisit the text to check your answers.
- After you have answered their questions, ask students to close their books so that they can try to answer your questions.
- When the questioning period is over and questions have been answered, clarified, reformatted, or discarded, students can use the questions and answers to make predictions for the remaining reading.

Christine's students participated in ReQuest after reading chapter 15, "Getting Rich Quickly," in *War, Peace, and All That Jazz*. Hector's questions are presented in Figure 2.2. As you can see, Hector has taken some notes on his questions to check to make sure Christine has answered correctly. His prediction is that the rest of their reading is going to be related to the Stock Market, the crash, and what happened to all the people who lost all their money. He'll now continue reading the chapter to see if his predictions are

1. What is the stock exchange: Organized system for sharing and buying shares.

2. In what
Exact date the New York reached record levels : September 24th 1929.

3. Why would the investors would not have enegh cash to pay off the loans : Dificult to pay to pay.

4. When did the investors start selling their stocks : late September

5. What date is Black thursday : is october 24 , a day that the panic began.

Figure 2.2 Hector's Questions

accurate and what new information he can gain to answer his questions. This activity has helped Hector make meaning from the text by using conversation and connections.

Code Breaker: Learning How to Learn Specialized Language

As we attempt to help students overcome the language barriers to content literacy, word study is always an important aspect of our instruction. Baker, Simmons and Kameenui suggest that "The relation between reading comprehension and vocabulary knowledge is strong and unequivocal. Although the causal direction of the relations is not understood clearly, there is evidence that the relation is largely reciprocal" (1995, 36). Word study instruction can be used to support comprehension in three broad areas: building content language awareness, teaching specialized vocabulary words necessary for understanding current reading, and providing students with strategies for understanding new and unknown words in their independent reading.

Content Language Awareness

Christine fosters content language awareness each day as she reads to and with her students from a wide variety of texts (see Appendix D). Her students are immersed in the language of history, and the words that are important to them and their study are recorded so that they have access to these words to support their reading and writing. She uses the approaches of read aloud and shared reading to build background knowledge, make connections to history, and develop an awareness of language connected to the history they are studying. The words on the word wall Figure 1.6, for example, were collected as the class studied the colonies and the American Revolution. After finishing this unit, they will begin a unit on war. Students will examine the words currently on the word wall, decide which ones they think would still be appropriate in a unit on war, and then take the others down, leaving space for new words they will discover in the new study. The door of a storage closet (see the photograph in Figure 2.3) makes an additional place for students to collect words that represent new terms they learn during the current unit.

For most students, just collecting the words is not enough to allow them to understand and retain the words for later retrieval and use. Words have to be integrated into students' worlds by connecting them to areas in which they

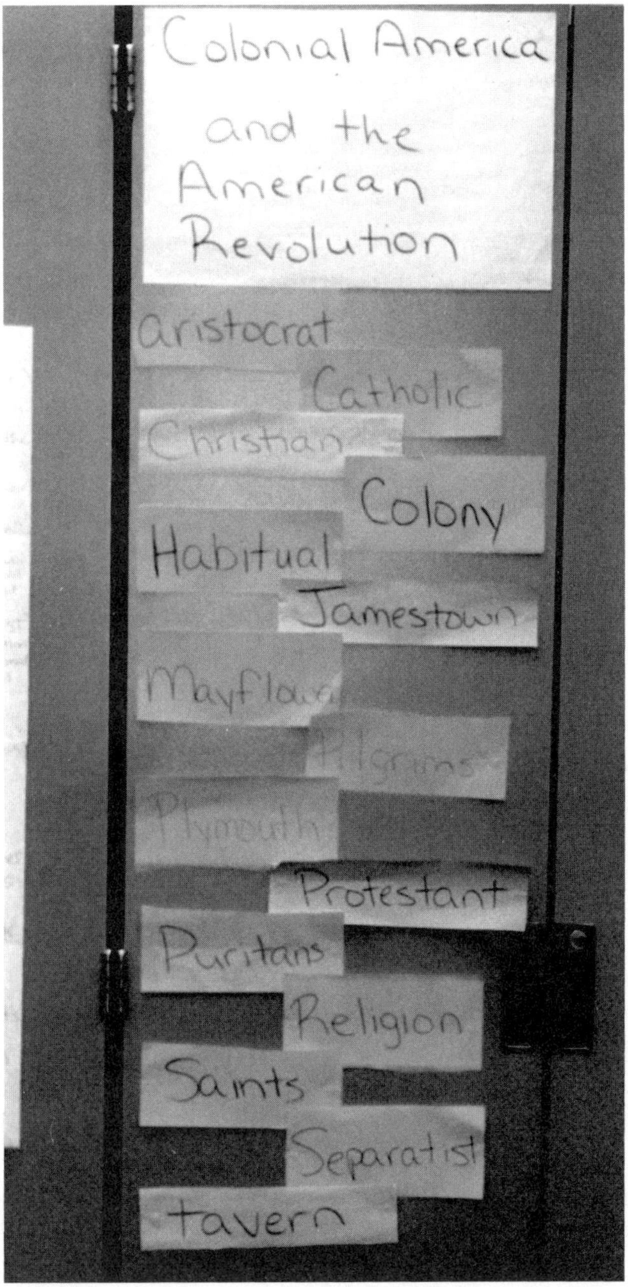

Figure 2.3 Word Wall on Closet Door

already have some understanding. Having to apply words in meaningful ways increases the chances that students will retain them for later use.

One way that content word meanings can be reinforced is by asking students to apply, explain, and illustrate their content words in their academic journals. This can be done with students responding to any of the following Word Illumination writing prompts:

- Explain the word so that a friend could understand its meaning.
- Describe how this word would be used in a specific time, place, event, or situation.
- Choose one of the characters or historical figures we have encountered and write some dialogue for a scene where that person would use this word.
- List other words someone might use in place of this word.
- Make a prediction for a situation in which someone might use this word.
- Write about a personal connection you have with this word.
- Write a question that this word would answer.
- Use this word in a news headline and then write the first paragraph for the headline that shows why the word was in the headline.
- Illustrate the word's meaning and then illustrate its opposite.
- If you saw this word on a sign, what would your next action be?

Students enjoy the creative aspect of showing you they know the word, its context, and application; this exercise makes the words more meaningful and memorable.

Exclusion Brainstorming

Exclusion Brainstorming (Blachowicz, 1986) is an instructional strategy that helps students build word banks of words related to the specific content you are studying. After having students read, view, or study an event, topic, concept or time period, give students a list of words and ask them to think critically about the words in the list. They could use this activity as a prewriting strategy by examining the words for three purposes: excluding words that would not make sense in a piece of writing about this topic or event, circling for inclusion those words that fit the event or context, and adding to the list related words that members of the group put forth in the course of their discussion.

The list of words in Figure 2.4 represents an exclusion brainstorming connected to the students' study of the Depression (chapters 15–17 in *War, Peace*

The Great Depression

Discuss the words in the box below with members of your group. Taking the role of a news reporter, decide which of these words you would use in your article and which you would exclude from your article.

shanty	events	lazy
shares	funds	pretend
millions	streets	banks
newspaper	television	savings
deduct	harmony	unemployed
management	census	economy
President	prevented	shack
happiness	prosperous	dream
wasteful	taxes	

Based on your group discussion, what other critical words would you now add to the ones you chose from the list above?

_____   _____

_____   _____

_____   _____

(Adapted from Blachowicz, 1986)

Figure 2.4 Exclusion Brainstorming

and All That Jazz, A History of US, Book 9). Students worked with group members, discussing the words and talking about which words might fit the writing they planned to do. In this process, they are able to figure out new and unknown words, clarify word meanings by revisiting the text, and determine which content words fit their writing purpose.

Teaching Specialized Vocabulary Words

Some words are so critical to students' understanding that we teach those words directly, giving students multiple opportunities to see each word in use. Graves and Graves (1994) make a distinction between teaching vocabulary and teaching concept. Teaching vocabulary occurs when you provide new labels for words connected to an already familiar concept. For example, if your students knew the concept of intolerance, you are teaching vocabulary by labeling and connecting bias and prejudice to the concept of intolerance. If, on the other hand, students had no understanding of the concept, then you would have to offer several experiences with the concept word before you could add other vocabulary words to that concept. Given the challenges of teaching both critical vocabulary words and new concepts, this is often the place where you might use a graphic organizer in order to make the abstract concept more concrete.

In the example shown in Figure 2.5, Christine has adapted the Words in Context graphic organizer (Allen, 1999) by deleting the cells for non-examples and adding cells for students to list word parts they recognize and other words in the same word family. Her target word is the concept of *revolution*. She has chosen this word because the class has just begun a unit on the American Revolution. As they read their textbooks and the supplemental texts Christine reads to them (see Appendix D for a complete listing), they return to their graphic organizer to add to their knowledge base about the concept. They are highlighting aspects of the concept's definition, creating lists of words that are from the same family, and making connections to other revolutions.

When Christine and her students were studying the Civil Rights Movement, she realized that they using many words interchangeably, as if there were no differences in their meanings. Her assessment led her to create a word study that built on previous word studies and solidified their understandings of the distinctions among three words: *racism, prejudice,* and *anti-Semitism.* For this word, she has used the graphic Alike but Different (Allen, 2002). From Figure 2.6, we can see that students have used what they learned

Words In Context Plus

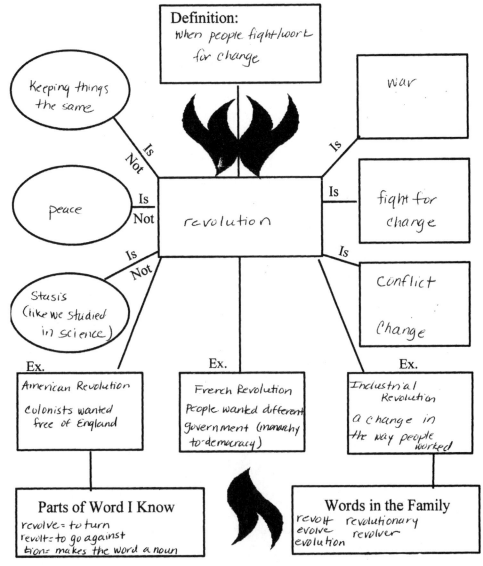

Definition:
When people fight/work
for change

Keeping things
the same

Is
Not

war

peace

Is
Not

Is

revolution

Is

fight for
change

Is
Not

Is

Stasis
(like we studied
in science)

Conflict

Change

Ex.

American Revolution
Colonists wanted
free of England

Ex.

French Revolution
People wanted different
government (monarchy
to democracy)

Ex.

Industrial
Revolution
a change in
the way people
worked

Parts of Word I Know
revolve = to turn
revolt = to go against
tion = makes the word a noun

Words in the Family
revolt   revolutionary
evolve   revolver
evolution

Figure 2.5 Graphic Organizer, Adapted

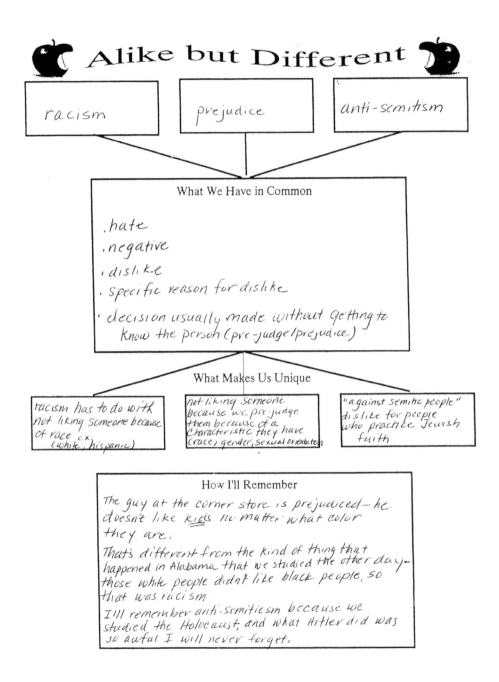

Alike but Different

racism	prejudice	anti-semitism

What We Have in Common

- hate
- negative
- dislike
- specific reason for dislike
- decision usually made without getting to know the person (pre-judge/prejudice)

What Makes Us Unique

racism has to do with not liking someone because of race ex; (white, hispanic)	not liking someone because we pre-judge them because of a characteristic they have (race, gender, sexual orientation)	"against semitic people" dislike for people who practice Jewish faith

How I'll Remember

The guy at the corner store is prejudiced—he doesn't like <u>kids</u> no matter what color they are.

That's different from the kind of thing that happened in Alabama that we studied the other day—those white people didn't like black people, so that was racism.

I'll remember anti-semiticism because we studied the Holocaust, and what Hitler did was so awful I will never forget.

Figure 2.6 Alike but Different Organizer

in their study of the Holocaust as well as information from the current unit to refine their understanding of these three terms.

Using and adapting graphic organizers to meet the needs of students is common practice when teaching content vocabulary. The "sea of talk" that surrounds the completing of the graphic makes the word more memorable for most students. When students add connections from their current reading and study and their own lives as a support to help them remember the word, they are more likely to recognize the word in their reading and use the word in their writing.

Strategies for Learning New and Unknown Words

We can't possibly teach students every new and unknown word they may encounter as they read history. Nor can we anticipate which words they won't know or which words they will be able to ignore because they are relatively unimportant in terms of comprehension. Gallagher and Pearson point out the fallacy in thinking that it is possible or desirable to teach all content words prior to reading: "If the passages are either too familiar or too unfamiliar to a given group of students, vocabulary instruction may be redundant or else too sparse to eliminate strong background knowledge weakness" (1983, 327).

A better instructional option is teaching students multiple ways for figuring out new and unknown words when they encounter them. When we involve students in how to figure out words, we are teaching them a strategy. If the strategy lesson works, the reader will have this strategy at a conscious level, ready to use as the need arises. Additionally, the strategy should be transferable to any type of text or any context.

The word-learning strategy readers use most often is simply skipping the word, but that can be problematic when students are reading history. Struggling readers who skip every word they don't know, will read and comprehend very few words. Giving students strategy instruction on how to figure out new and unknown words by using a variety of context clues, actually moves them toward becoming independent word learners. Although context, when used in isolation, is an unreliable source of word meaning (Baumann and Kameenui, 1991), students can actually figure out many new words if we teach context in a broader sense.

Context can be defined as local (the rest of the words in the sentence) or global (all of the other information we have to figure out the unknown word.) Context is based on using clues to figure out new or unfamiliar words.

The graphic organizer shown in Figure 2.7 can help students understand the various places they can look for these context clues. First, we have helped students put the process of using context clues in their own words. Then, we have given students the opportunity to test out several different kinds of context clues: background knowledge (clues in their heads), local context (clues within the sentence), word parts (clues inside the word), and global context (clues on the surrounding pages, such as title, genre, pictures, foot/endnotes, graphs, and maps). As students encounter these kinds of context clues in their reading, we note them under the space provided for examples in the graphic organizer. The examples make the strategy lesson more memorable.

These three types of code breaking all support reading comprehension. The more words we know related to the reading we do, the easier it is to comprehend and the more likely we are to remember what we read. Pearson and Taylor's research study *Teaching Reading: Effective Schools, Accomplished Teachers*, found support for the intentional teaching we have described: "Effective teachers expect and encourage their students to use the skills they learn in a self-regulated fashion, with teachers explaining to and modeling for students how to coordinate multiple strategies (e.g., Attempt to recognize words by using phonics, word chunks, and semantic context clues)" (2002, 365). Building content word banks, teaching specialized vocabulary, and teaching students how to figure out words on their own provide an effective foundation for word study in reading history.

Text User: Examining and Managing Text Types

Adept and motivated readers have internalized ways to manage the reading task when given assignments from their textbooks. They know how to use the supports that are in texts and they know how and when to employ that knowledge to help them comprehend a text even if they don't find the text interesting. Struggling and/or unmotivated readers often have no idea how to manage the reading experience and so do not even attempt to complete reading assignments.

McKenna, Kear, and Randolphe's study of children's attitudes toward reading, report on the connection between past experience and attitude: "Attitudes are formed in part on the basis of beliefs about the outcomes of reading. It is natural to predict that poorer readers, who have reason to expect frustrating outcomes, will tend to harbor more negative attitudes than better readers" (1995, 941). Such historical lack of success with textbooks influences

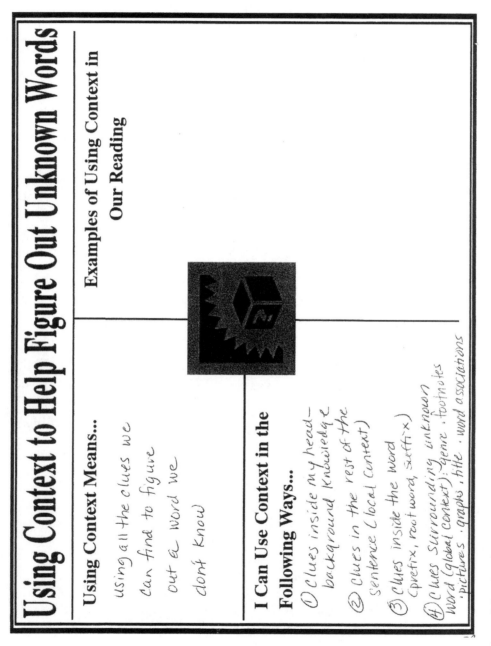

Using Context to Help Figure Out Unknown Words

Using Context Means...

using all the clues we can find to figure out a word we don't know

Examples of Using Context in Our Reading

I Can Use Context in the Following Ways...

1. Clues inside my head—background knowledge
2. Clues in the rest of the sentence (local context)
3. Clues inside the word (prefix, root word, suffix)
4. Clues surrounding unknown word (global context): genre · footnotes · pictures · graphs · title · word associations

Figue 2.7 Graphic Organizer for Context Clues

students' attitudes toward all subsequent textbook experiences. Often the biggest challenge with these students is not that they don't finish their work; it is that they usually don't even begin. Each reading experience is seen as a new and impossible task, because they have not learned to use the consistent and predictable supports that would help them determine main ideas, develop an understanding of critical concepts, find patterns in events or historical acts, and store that knowledge for future reading.

This knowledge leads us to the first stage of instruction in supporting readers as "Text Users," which is teaching students how to read a variety of text types. There are three broad types of text: expository, functional, and narrative. Each type of text has its own purpose and its own text supports that help meet the goal of that purpose. In a journal article, Roger Farr cited the importance of teaching students how to read all types of texts: "Good reading instruction focuses the attention of readers by teaching them what to expect from different kinds of texts, how those texts can fulfill their needs (their purposes for reading), and the strategies for constructing the meaning they need from particular kinds of texts" (2003, 3). In history classes, we use all three types of texts in order to provide students with multiple points of view; therefore, we need to teach students how to read all three types in the course of their time with us.

Expository Texts

The purpose of an expository text is to provide information to increase the reader's knowledge of a subject or an event. Expository writing includes texts such as encyclopedia entries, textbooks, political analyses, and front-page news articles. In my research (Allen, 1995), students reported that reading their textbooks was the most challenging reading they did in school. Christine's students cited the following reasons why reading their textbooks was difficult:

- Too many unknown words
- We don't know who the people are in the reading
- Not quite interesting (well, it's really boring)
- We don't have enough background knowledge

As with our discussion of how to learn new and unknown words, students have to learn how to read expository texts such as their textbooks. One important step in teaching strategies for reading this text type is teaching students how to use text supports to aid in comprehension. Text supports are there to help us access, organize, and understand content. Text supports include the following:

- Title
- Headings
- Subheadings
- Diagrams
- Pictures
- Graphs
- Charts
- Legends
- Keys
- Timelines
- First paragraph
- Last paragraph
- Introductions
- Captions
- Font styles (bold, italics, color)
- Focus questions
- Objectives
- Glossary
- Table of contents
- Appendices
- Index
- Marginal notes

When teaching our students how and when to use these supports, we have to help them locate the supports and understand the purpose of each one. One effective method is to use a textbook scavenger hunt for supports. To demonstrate this strategy lesson, we have used two pages (pages 12 and 13) from *The First Americans (A History of US,* Book 1) (see Figure 2.8) as an example of expository writing. These two pages form the basis of a model lesson on how to use text supports to help students read.

After students have read the two pages from this textbook, we supplied a blank template (see Figure 2.9) that students could use to identify and label the supports they found on these pages.

As students worked in pairs to discover the supports in the text, they were able to locate title, marginal notes, timeline, pictures, captions, drawings and

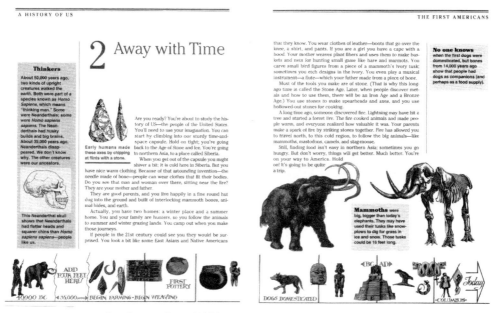

Figure 2.8   Sample of Expository Writing

vocabulary words. After students labeled the template with these terms, we used the template and the text to discuss the purpose of each support and how that support could help them comprehend future textbook assignments. Students then created a record of these supports (see Text-to-Text graphic in Appendix A) and their purposes. The example in Figure 2.10 shows how a student, Christopher, used the form to document each support and its purpose and gave examples of the supports in use in a new chapter he is currently reading in his textbook.

At this point, students have discovered, discussed, and made notes about when and how to use these text supports. If we want to know whether they truly understand the strategy of using text supports, we have to set up situations in which students use the supports in order to access the content in their textbooks.

Textbook Activity Guide

One of the most effective ways I have found to reinforce strategy lessons on text supports is to use a Textbook Activity Guide (Davey, 1986). A Textbook Activity Guide (TAG) is created to uncover the content in a text-

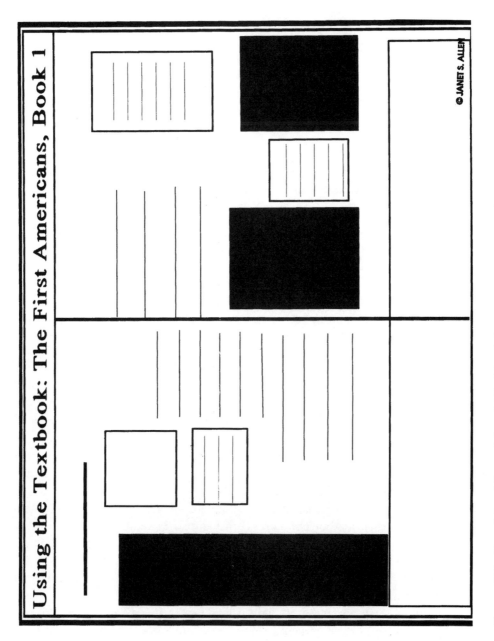

Using the Textbook: The First Americans, Book 1

© JANET S. ALLEN

Figure 2.9   Template of Pages 14 and 15 of Book 1

Text support or feature	Text: American Journey	Text: Making 13 Colonies	Chris Darrow 9-23-02 Period #4
Non-Fiction	Writing: leaves out smaller details; facts organized by date.	Writing: more details in a story~like manner — this is like narrative text.	
Title and subtitle	text stands out, more of them, tell you the main idea of text.	text stands out, no subtitles, tell you main idea of text.	
Pictures and Captions	gives the reader a look at what the text is talking about, help you locate what youre reading about.	→ Same	
Important facts/ Questions	Questions come at the end, important of interesting facts are on first page.	some question on side, some in paragraph. Interesting facts are in captions or on side.	
Bold Italics vocabulary	vocab. words are in paragraphs; definitions in glossary.	vocab. words and definitions are on side.	

Figure 2.10   Christopher's Documentation of Text Supports

book chapter and to reinforce whatever strategy you have just taught your students. In this case, as we have taught students how to use text supports, the guide focuses on students using those supports to access content, develop an understanding for content language, make connections and predictions, and summarize and synthesize information.

Students work with partners to complete the TAG by using the strategy codes and their textbooks. The TAG in Figure 2.11 reinforces the use of text supports in each one of the prompts for three chapters they are studying in *The First Americans*. When creating a TAG, we always try to make the TAGs interactive to engage students in making the content personally meaningful, while reinforcing the power of using text supports.

Our ultimate goal is that students will no longer need a TAG in order to complete their reading assignments. Flood, Lapp, and Wood note that our goal is to make the guides unnecessary: "Bear in mind that study guides are only a step-

Textbook Activity Guide for <u>The First Americans</u>, Chapter 23, Chapter 31, and Chapter 32.
Please use pages 111-113, 138-139, 140-143 to complete the following questions.

1. Skim page 111. Ponce de Leon sailed north from Puerto Rico in 1513. What was he looking for, and what did he find instead?

To find Kindom of Gold but he found New land (Florida)

2. Look at the pictures and their captions on pages 111-113. Write two sentences about Incan culture and the effect of Spanish exploration on the Incas.

Incans eat to much meat
The Incans fought to save their city from Pizzaro

3. According to the purple boxes on pages 111 and 112, what element attracted the Spanish to explore the New World?

-land of Gold

4. Read the last sentence on page 113. Do you think this is true? Why or why not?

No, cause you need to Comunicate

5. The last few sentences on page 139 say, "Looking back, today, it seems as if people and nations were acting just like silly little kids. Each one was saying, 'My religion is better than yours.' Actually, each believed God was on his side."
Please read pages 138-139 and explain what the author means by these statements.

The author means we should'int fight because of different religion.

6. Re-read those sentences from #5, and think about what you read on those two pages. How do those past events relate to what is happening in our world today, for example, with the attack on the Twin Towers and the Pentagon?

They way they relate is because the religion we are relating because the Attaked our building

7. Read the first two paragraphs on page 140. Why do you think the Italian explorers like Christopher Columbus had their names changed from the Italian spelling to a more "English" spelling? Who were the three Italian sailors that helped lead Europeans to the New World, and what countries hired them?

Some can't pronounse there names

8. Read the yellow box about privateers. How is that different from what you know about pirates? How is it similar to what you already knew?

They have a different names they both do the same thing which is stealing

9. Read the last two paragraphs on page 143. How did the stories of these French sailors affect the settlement of America? Were the stories truthful? How would you feel if you sailed all the way to the New World after listening to these stories, and discovered the truth?

I whant because would line Some Jewls

Figure 2.11 Activity Guide with Strategy Codes

ping stone to independent learning. Once students have mastered a learning strategy using a study guide, it's important to teach them how to apply that strategy on their own. *A major goal of study guides is to make their use obsolete"* (1992, 4; emphasis in original). We will know that students have internalized the structure of expository texts when they can insert any text supports that are missing.

When Christine's students read the chapter on the Revolutionary War in *From Colonies to Country*, (*A History of US*, Book 3) she was able to assess whether students had internalized the supports. Students discovered that there were no subtitles to help guide their reading. Christine asked them to break the chapter into paragraphs, read the paragraphs, and create subtitles for those paragraphs. As a way to reinforce what they had learned, she noted with them that when they turn their subtitles into questions, they should be able to find the answer to each question in the paragraph that follows each subtitle. Alisha's list of subtitles, shown in Figure 2.12, demonstrates her ability to create subtitles; her responses to questions at the end of class (exit slips) (bottom of Figure 2.12) showed Christine that she also understood the function of subtitles in expository texts.

In Costa and Kallick's book *Assessing and Reporting on Habits of Mind*, the authors discuss the importance of students developing and using the habit of thinking about thinking throughout their lives. Students who have found success with this habit can list the steps for how they will solve a problem, and they can tell you where they are in the sequence of those steps. They trace the pathways and blind alleys they took on the road to a problem's solution. They describe what data are lacking, and they also describe their plans for producing the missing data. (2000, 5). With the use of process papers and exit slips, Christine is teaching her students the strength of metacognition (thinking about thinking). In so doing, she is making the strategy transferable to other texts that represent similar challenges.

Several weeks later, when Christine and her students moved to a research project, with each student choosing a war to research, she was able to revisit the use of text supports for a different purpose. She used the Content Brainstorming graphic organizer (Allen, 2002) to help her students see that supports can guide comprehension. Her lesson centered on the ways key words, subtitles, pictures, and captions can help students make connections, and predictions and generate questions that focus their reading. Each student completed the Content Brainstorming graphic by using the text supports in the chapter of the textbook that covered the war that student had chosen (see Figure 2.13). Each student then used the questions to guide his reading, looking for answers to those questions and generating new questions.

9/9

The Revolutionary war part II, or the war of 1812   Alisha
Chapman
11-13-02
P-3rd

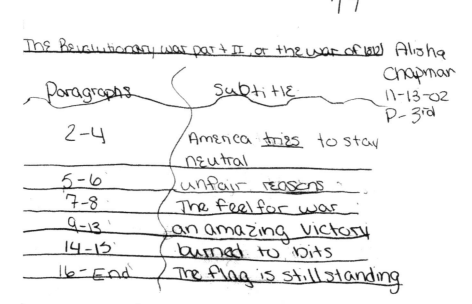

Paragraphs	Subtitle
2-4	America tries to stay neutral
5-6	unfair reasons
7-8	The feel for war
9-13	an amazing victory
14-15	burned to bits
16-End	The flag is still standing

1. How would these subtitles make the chapter easier to read? You could understand what your reading befor you read.

2 How did creating subtitles help you better understand the chapter? Explain. by reading a thinking over what the chapter said

3 What was hard about creating subtitles? It was hard to make a catchy saying.

Figure 2-12   Alisha's List of Subtitles and Answers to Questions

Content Brainstorming

Chapter Title: War with Mexico

Key Words	Headings	Subheadings
James K. Polk	Just titles - The Outbreak of the War	Conquering New Mexico & Cali...
Mexico City	Rising Tensions	The Failure New Mexico
Rio Grande		
Monterrey	American Attitudes toward the War	The End of the War
Nueces River		
Winfield Scott	Polk's War Plan	The Capture of Mexico City
Zachary Taylor		
Veracruz		

Picture Walk: What predictions can you make about contents based on visuals? In the boxes write a description of the pictures in your chapter.

The picture shows a case with men on their horses in uniform and soldiers in a row with uniform holding up the American Flag.

Caption: Case showing General Zachary Taylor

Picture shows Amer. soldier. He's wearing a long hat, uniform looks old fashion. Has a white belt over waist & chest and he has a gun that is very long.

Caption: American soldier

The map shows Cali. and Mexico. It shows routes American B. Mexico Scott's took, American victory, US Naval Blockade and Disputed area.

Caption: The Mexican War 1846-1848 (Map)

Connections & Questions

What predictions & connections could you make about what you will learn in the chapter based on above text supports?

In this chapter I think I will read about
How the war came about and why it where did it happen and who was involved

What questions could you ask that would focus and guide your reading?

Questions I have before I read
Why did the war happen?
How many people died?

Figure 2.13   Content Brainstorming Graphic Organizer

Functional Texts

Functional texts are structured to help readers get somewhere or accomplish a task. Maps, schedules, diagrams, directions, and warning labels are all examples of functional texts. In teaching students how to read functional texts, we focus again on the text supports that help us read this kind of text. A model lesson can occur when we use a map such as the one from pages 70–71 in *From Colonies to Country (A History of Us:* Book 3) (see Figure 2.14) and a map of the state in which our students live.

Students, working in learning groups, should compare and contrast the two maps by discussing the following points:

- How do the two maps differ? (content, supports, style)
- What can you determine about the purpose of each of the maps?
- Could the maps have multiple purposes?
- How do the legends and keys differ? How are they similar?
- After studying the maps, what questions do you have?

Using students' responses to these prompts, we can them help them create steps they would use in order to read a map, document these steps for predictable patterns, and see that some maps may have idiosyncratic elements or supports. This exercise reinforces the transferable strategy of reading a functional text. Steps that would come out of a lesson on how to read expository texts (here, maps) would probably include the following:

- Determine my purpose for reading the map.
- Examine the legends and keys.
- Learn how to interpret charts and graphs (mileage, highways).
- Use the compass to help with directions.
- Analyze types of roads and determine which roads fit my purpose for reading the map.
- Make sense of any inserts.
- Note topographical features I might need to know.
- Read highway markers.

Narrative Texts

Narrative texts tell the reader a story. We believe this is one of the reasons we have had so much success in using *A History of Us* with our students; history has come alive for them because much of this expository text uses a narrative

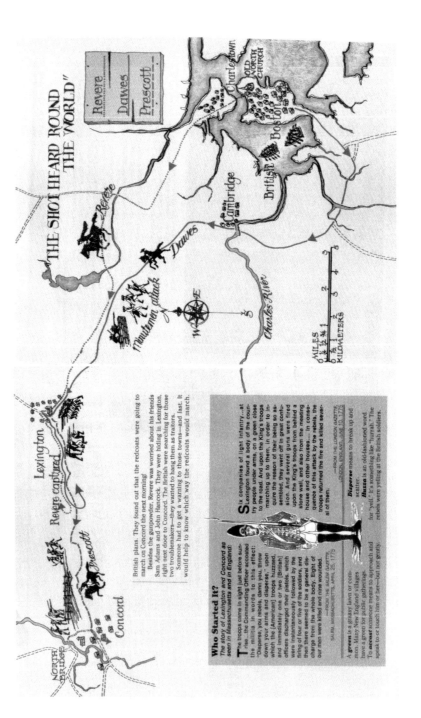

Figure 2.14 Map

nonfiction format. Narrative texts can take many forms: poetry, drama, novel, short story, or narrative nonfiction. Regardless of the form, narrative texts share the common characteristic of story features. Students expect the features of story in a short story or a novel, but often forget or ignore those features in a narrative poem. Since many students say that poetry is difficult for them to read, examining the features of story in a poem is one way to reinforce some of the supports that might make a narrative poem understandable for them. To illustrate this type of text, I have used Sara Holbrook's very powerful narrative poem "Naked" (*Chicks Up Front*, 1998).

Naked

The first time I saw a man naked,
it was not my brother.
I was born without a brother,
which everyone knows
is like being born without green hair,
or a wart on the tip of your nose,
or the skin of a reptile.
Being born with no brother was a definite asset,
or so I thought until fifth grade, when I started to wonder.
I wondered why every time I would mention the word "it,"
in any context,
the boys would laugh—they'd fall on the ground.
Likewise, if I would say the word "them,"
in any context, the boys would laugh—they'd fall on the ground.
It was as if we were tuned into two different programs,
like they were tuned into cartoons
and I was watching a mystery.
I wondered.
And I wondered with the sense of urgency
of 4:30 in the afternoon and Mom says,
"No more snacks before dinner,"
and you're starving.
I wanted what I wanted and I wanted it now.
Prevailing neighborhood trade policies
provided for such things,
a look for a look, even up.
Worth considering,
Until a permission slip came home from school.
There was to be a film about growing up.
Well, even I knew that was fiftiespeak for "naked."
My wonder swelled within me—
I had swallowed a balloon.
I couldn't breathe.

Breathless, until the film showed us diagrams.
Diagrams? Bones without the meat.
It looked like a direction sheet on how to assemble a bicycle.
Absolutely no help at all. I deflated gradually.
A couple weeks later, another film.
No permission slip this time.
Just a film about the war of our fathers, World War II.
Germany, Hitler youth. Wind up soldiers.
Waving train cars.
Pits of white, white limbs. Ovens, not for cakes.
Three men standing against a fence, heads shaved.
Their collar bones poking out like
coat hangers without the clothes.
The picture was cut off at the hollow places where their bellies belonged.
Except for one man, standing in the background,
who stepped deliberately to the side.
Stripped of any sense of wonder or urgency,
he made no attempt to cover himself.
He faced the camera because he wanted me to see.

I dragged my feet a little on the way
home from school that day,
kicking aimlessly at the fallen leaves.
Not so much in a hurry.
After all, I had seen.
For the first time,
I had seen a man,
Naked.

We certainly don't want to take away from the aesthetic experience of
this poem; we would want to read the poem and give students an opportunity to respond to the poem, its content, and its impact on their thinking before using it for a model lesson on reading narrative texts. After that
discussion, we can revisit the poem to examine the supports explicitly
or subtly used in this poem that are characteristic of narrative text
structure.

As part of this lesson, we could also read a short story to students and
ask them to identify the elements of story found in the short story.
Students will quickly come up with features of story such as title, characters, setting, plot, conflict, dialogue, theme, and story grammar (begin-
ning/middle/end). We ask students to work together to determine how
those elements help them read a short story. We can examine how
Holbrook used those same elements in her narrative poem by using the
following steps:

- Use the title to predict content, ask questions, and make connections prior to reading the poem.
- Look for the features of story:
  Who are the characters? How are we introduced to the characters?
  What is the setting? How did Sara help us figure that out without using lengthy descriptive passages?
  Is there a plot? How is a plot communicated in such a short text? Could we make a timeline of the plot events?
  Where is the conflict? How do we come to understand the conflict? How is the conflict resolved—or is it?
  Is the dialogue obvious or subtle? How do you know when someone is speaking?
  What is the theme? Do you determine theme in a narrative poem the same way you would in a short story or novel?
  How is tone communicated? What does this say about the use of language in a narrative poem?
  Can we determine story grammar [beginning, middle, end] even in a poem?
- Now, take some time to think about how the story structure helped you experience the spirit and the content of the poem.
- What can you take away from this experience with reading narrative texts that you could use the next time you independently read a narrative text?

For many of you, this type of strategy lesson would take away from the beauty of the text. For most of our readers, this type of lesson has to happen for them to understand how we approach texts. Gallagher and Pearson noted that Hansen and Pearson's research conclude that "younger and older poor readers benefit from explicit attempts to alter comprehension strategies; older good readers, on the other hand, did not seem to benefit nearly so much, perhaps because they have developed adequate strategies on their own" (1983, 330). When using diverse texts with our students in history classes, it is critical that we model for students how we read those texts rather than just assigning them to be read.

Connecting Solid Foundations and Comprehension

The comprehension strategies we highlight in this chapter are effective only when combined with the strategies demonstrated in the first chapter. There is a solid connection between interest in reading and the use of strategies; each time we create an opportunity to make reading history interesting, we increase the chances that subsequent reading will be comprehended. The research of Guthrie, Alao, and Rinehart on engagement highlights this connection:

> The deep processing strategies needed for learning depend heavily on intrinsic motivation. Intrinsic motivations, including interest in content, wanting to learn for its own sake, and feeling immersed in literacy tasks are associated with more frequent use of strategies for reading. In contrast, extrinsic motivations consist of competition, avoidance of negative evaluation, and the desire to obtain rewards, grades, and social approval. These extrinsic motivations lead to reading avoidance and the use of weak strategies. (1997, 439)

Students' comprehension in reading history will depend largely on our ability to get them engaged, interested, and wanting to know more. When students are interested and engaged, when they can comprehend a variety of texts written from multiple perspectives, they can transfer and extend that content knowledge to other historical events and to their lives.

Chapter 3

Making Learning Meaningful
Extending and Transferring Knowledge after Reading

Perhaps the most important way in which we strive to integrate our classrooms and curriculum is to draw the lives of our students into the center of what we do. We organize our work to integrate the classroom content and the lives of our students so that they can recognize the relevance of the content, and so that they can bring their experiences and interests to the learning.

Lindquist and Selwyn (2000, 19)

When encouraging readers of history, we have several broad goals for our students as readers and as learners. We want them to leave their reading with some knowledge of content and to be able to discriminate among ideas for significance, bias, point of view, and perspective. We would like them to think about what they learned and how they learned it, acknowledging the value of talk and others' opinions and ideas when they are forming their own opinions. We would also hope the study we've done would prompt them to ask new questions that lead them to further reading and study.

At this stage in their lives, these readers have assumed the reader role of "Text Critic" as they analyze, synthesize, apply, and extend their learning into independent learning and historical expertise. Many of us have enjoyed students who see themselves as historical experts. On Christine's first day as a social studies teacher, before the bell had rung to allow students to enter class, she encountered her first expert in her new students, Stephen:

> "So, you're going to be my U.S. History teacher. What do you know about Patton?"

"Do you mean George Patton from World War II?"

"Yes. If you're going to expect me to learn from you, you better know your World War II stuff. And, you're going to have to have seen the movie. Have you seen it?"

"Well, no. But if you have it . . .

"I have it right here with me. Watch it tonight and we can talk about it tomorrow."

Christine had found her first expert—and her first ally. This is the kind of student we hope we foster as we are planning curriculum and instruction throughout the year. In *Ways That Work: Putting Social Studies Standards into Practice,* Tarry Lindquist expects these outcomes and plans for them at the beginning of the unit. "Whenever I plan a unit, I first brainstorm ways my students can acquire knowledge, manipulate data, practice skills, and apply their understanding through group activities" (1997, 101). As a result of the time Christine and her students spend working on questioning, thoughtful and careful reading, exposure to multiple texts, and sharing ideas with others, the satisfaction of those goals is evident in her classroom.

Students in Christine's classroom analyzed history and their thinking about history every day as they applied their knowledge of how historical information is communicated from one generation or group to another. As I travel from school to school, I see hundreds of great examples of how students have extended and transferred the meaningful learning they have done in their history classes. In this chapter, we highlight the instructional strategies and activities that have had the greatest impact on students' extending and transferring history to their lives, their inquiry, and their views of the world.

The So-What Factor: Remembering Important Ideas

One way that we can help students transfer learning is by teaching them how to record information and ideas in ways that make information memorable and accessible. Christine had already worked with her students on the difference between primary information and secondary information when she decided to support them in learning how to take notes that would make sense to them at a later time. Building that background, she showed students forms of note taking by which they could to record information that represented both big ideas and the secondary information supporting those big ideas. Three forms are highlighted in the following text: outlines/story maps, mapping/webbing, and R.E.A.P.

Outlines/Story Maps

In studying the Civil War, the students had read together "Dinner at Brown's Hotel" from *War, Terrible War (A History of US,* Book 6). After reading, students worked together to choose what they considered the most important events in what they had just read. Figure 3.1 represents the work of one pair of students who chose three big ideas: "The nation was in trouble," "Dinner at Brown's Hotel," and "Messages from dinner spreading." They listed information that supported each of those big ideas, using an outlining format.

When the outlines were finished, Chris talked with her students about making outlines that were memorable. She noted with them that the points listed on the outline had to be descriptive enough to trigger their memories

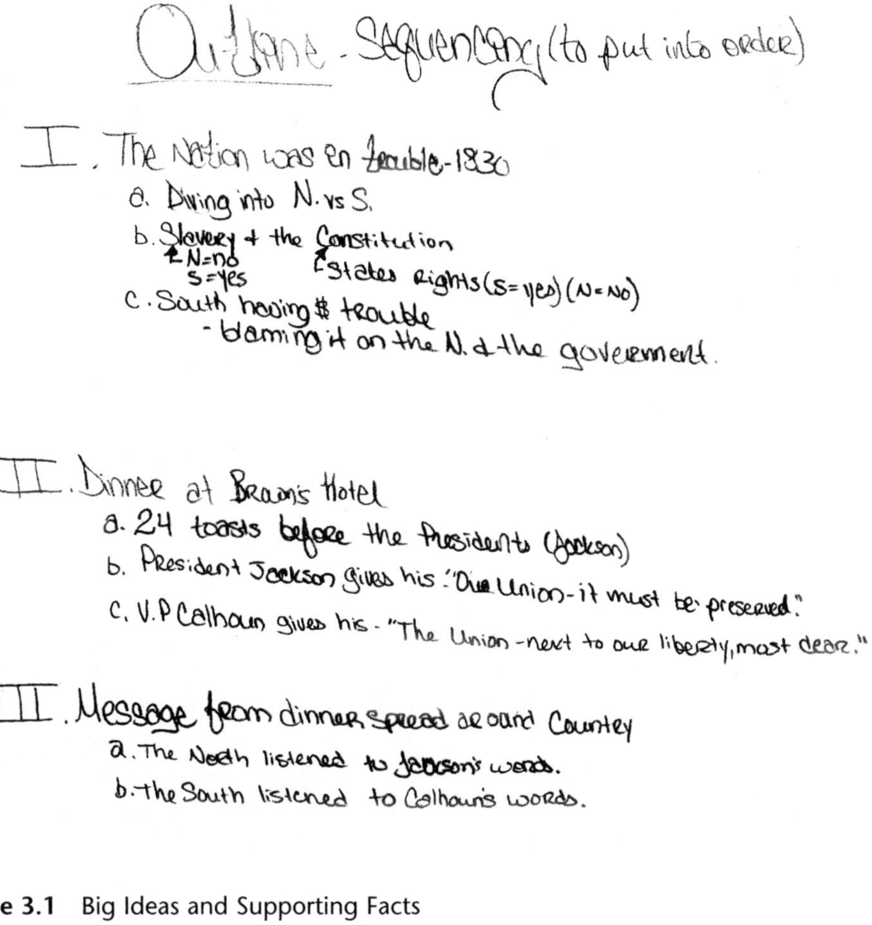

Outline - Sequencing (to put into order)

I. The Nation was in trouble - 1830
   a. Diving into N. vs S.
   b. Slavery + the Constitution
     N=no
     S=yes   States Rights (S=yes) (N=No)
   c. South having $ trouble
     - blaming it on the N. & the government.

II. Dinner at Brown's Hotel
   a. 24 toasts before the Presidents (Jackson)
   b. President Jackson gives his "Our Union - it must be preserved."
   c. V.P Calhoun gives his - "The Union - next to our liberty, most dear."

III. Message from dinner spread around Country
   a. The North listened to Jackson's words.
   b. The South listened to Calhoun's words.

Figure 3.1 Big Ideas and Supporting Facts

of the supporting details and the connections among the details and the main ideas from the reading. As a way to reinforce that descriptive/visual quality, she asked students to use their outlines to create story maps. Students could then go back to their outlines and add anything they believed necessary to making their outlines descriptive enough to be memorable. A student sample of a visual outline is shown in Figure 3.2.

Mapping/Webbing

Gallagher and Pearson are two of the many researchers who have noted the importance of mapping in extending students' understanding of the texts they read. "Students who do mapping are forced to deal with the structure of the author's text; however, and more importantly, they are forced to try to make connections among ideas even when the author has not explicitly specified those connections" (1983, 329). Maps can help students organize ideas and opinions, make connections among informational pieces, record information, make abstract concepts more concrete, and compare and contrast multiple texts.

Christine and her students have been studying the Constitution and the issues its framers were grappling with as they wrote the Constitution. As part of the reading they did while thinking about and discussing what the framers of the Constitution could have done with the slavery issue, Christine did a shared reading of "Good Words and Bad" *From Colonies to Country* (*A History of US*, Book 3). Students then used the graphic organizer Looking at Our Options (Allen, 2000) to examine the dilemma, put forth the options available to the framers, and examine the consequences of each of these options (Figure 3.3). Mapping allows students to examine such options in an organized and logical manner.

R.E.A.P.

R.E.A.P. (Eanet and Manzo, 1976) is a more elaborate form of taking notes that helps students internalize and determine the importance of information in a reading assignment. R.E.A.P. stands for the following stages of reading and recording of ideas:

- R—Read on your own.
- E—Encode the test by putting the gist of what you read in your own words.

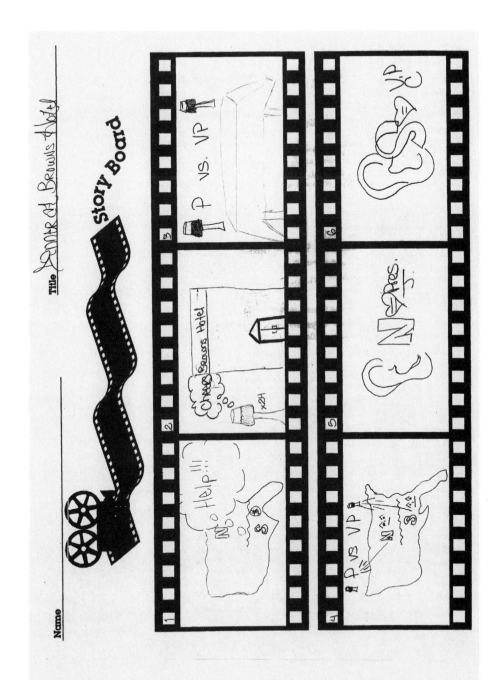

Figure 3.2 Visual Outline by Student

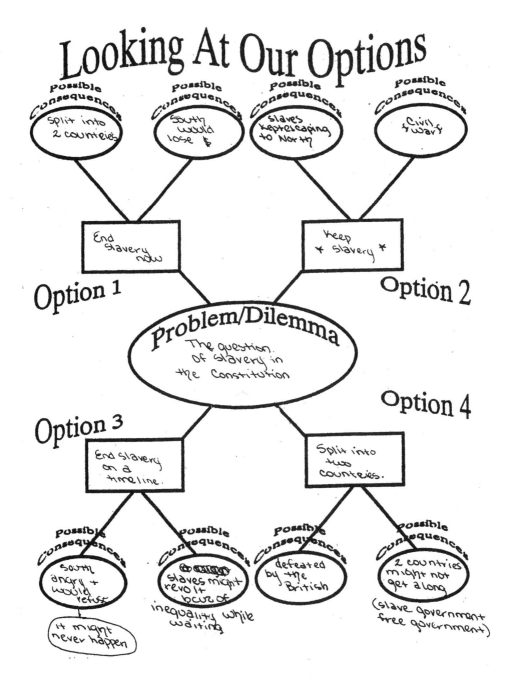

Figure 3.3 The Looking at Our Options Graphic Organizer

- A—Annotate the text by writing down the main ideas (notes, significant words, quotes) and the author's message.
- P—Ponder what you read by thinking and talking with others in order to make personal connections, develop questions about the topic, and/or connect this reading to other reading you have done.

R.E.A.P. is an excellent activity for students to note important information and to talk with others about connections and questions, as well as to establish purposes for further reading.

Christine's students used the R.E.A.P. strategy for taking notes, analyzing and questioning what they have learned so far about the Great Depression. Figure 3.4 shows that Stephanie has *read* and noted the title of the reading (R). She then *encoded* an important aspect of what she had read by defining "on margin" and drawing a diagram to help her remember how this concept works (E). She went on to *annotate* the information by writing down the main ideas behind the stock market crash (A) and, finally, to *ponder* what she has learned by summarizing what she knows and questioning what role the war played in this event (P). After each student had created an individual R.E.A.P., Christine was able to use the questions from their *ponder* sections to focus the class discussion. Students had an opportunity to clarify and add to their notes in this process.

Understanding Point of View and Multiple Perspectives

The National Social Studies Standards (Schneider, 1994) state that "Teachers of social studies at all school levels should provide developmentally appropriate experiences . . . identifying, describing, and evaluating multiple points of view" (1997). As we look at the problems our society faces—locally, nationally, and globally—because so many people are unable to view events or situations from multiple perspectives, we can see why this standard is a critical one. If we want students to begin to examine situations from multiple perspectives, we have to give them many opportunities to view the same event from different perspectives.

When I was teaching graduate teacher education classes, Christine was a student in one of the classes. An interesting event occurred during our fall semester. The Ku Klux Klan wanted to march in the holiday parade in one of our area communities. The board members argued the issue for several months. When they reached an impasse, they decided to cancel the parade rather than risk the tension and threatened lawsuits. My students and I spent

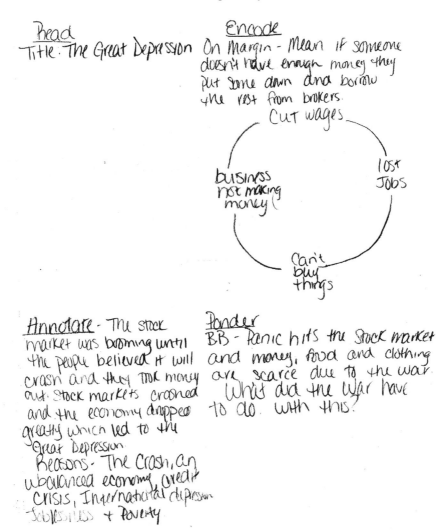

Figure 3.4 Stephanie's R.E.A.P.

some time listing the actual details of the event and then imagining how differently those events might have been recounted if told from a variety of perspectives.

We imagined a parent who had taken her son to marching band practice for several months, a member of the board who had argued the issue for several months, a KKK member who was fighting for his rights, the person who had arranged the parade for many years, and a local journalist all telling this

Figure 3.5

story. We came to realize that without changing the events that occurred, the way we communicated the story (quotes, tone, language, photographs) could make it seem as though these people had not been involved in the same event. As troubling as such discussions can be, our students need to engage in them to begin to view events from multiple perspectives. There are many ways to help students focus in order to have these important discussions; one of our most successful instructional strategies is highlighted here.

Multiple Sources: Multiple Perspectives

Providing students with multiple sources for information and description of the same event gives them an excellent opportunity to see how an event can be viewed in many ways. Blachowicz and Ogle cite the importance of this strategy: "Comparing how different authors handle the same topics or themes gives young readers a deeper understanding of and respect for point of view and perspective in human experience, as well as commonalities across cultures" (2001, 8). Knowing the value of teaching students to read and think while acknowledging and learning from the viewpoints of others is a critical component of Christine's teaching.

As a way of teaching multiple perspectives, Christine had her students use the graphic organizer Multiple Sources: Multiple Perspectives (Allen, 2000, 2002) to begin their study of the Vietnam conflict. All students began the study by searching their textbook: *All the People (A History of US,* Book 10). Each student then examined several supplemental sources related to Vietnam: letters, historical texts, and chronologies of important events in history (see Figure 3.6).

Christine had both an independent and a community purpose for this activity. First, she wanted to give students the opportunity to build background knowledge for their study. Second, she wanted them to be able to compare/contrast information and question how conflicting information could be presented on the same event. Finally, she wanted to use what she learned from their questions to help focus the remainder of their study. I once read a quote that said, "Whenever things sound easy, it turns out there's one part you didn't hear." That was the case with Christine's goals for this activity.

Christine reports,

> After reading our textbook chapter and thinking about the question of why the U. S. was involved in Vietnam, I brought out the packets I had put together with multiple perspectives on the events of the war. I asked my students to partner read them and use the Multiple Sources graphic to record information, infer by reading between the lines, and develop questions they wanted answered. Oddly enough, they had trouble figuring out what it meant to read between the lines. Then, I realized they were just copying irrelevant information and not asking any thoughtful questions. In period two, I thought it was a fluke; by period six, I knew I was doing something wrong.

> As I talked with the students, I realized that my purpose for the reading and the graphic organizer I had chosen did not particularly match up. I hadn't really looked past the name of the organizer (Multiple Sources: Multiple Perspectives) and so actually analyzed what students would be looking for as they attempted to fill out the columns. I wanted them to look at the different perspectives people had on the war and question why that might have occurred. The form led them to look for basic facts. It confused them with "reading between the lines," and it led them to base their questions on the facts they were finding instead of looking deeper.

> I regrouped the next day by asking students to tell me what they thought the title of the graphic organizer meant. They were able to tell me, so I asked them why looking at multiple perspectives might be important.

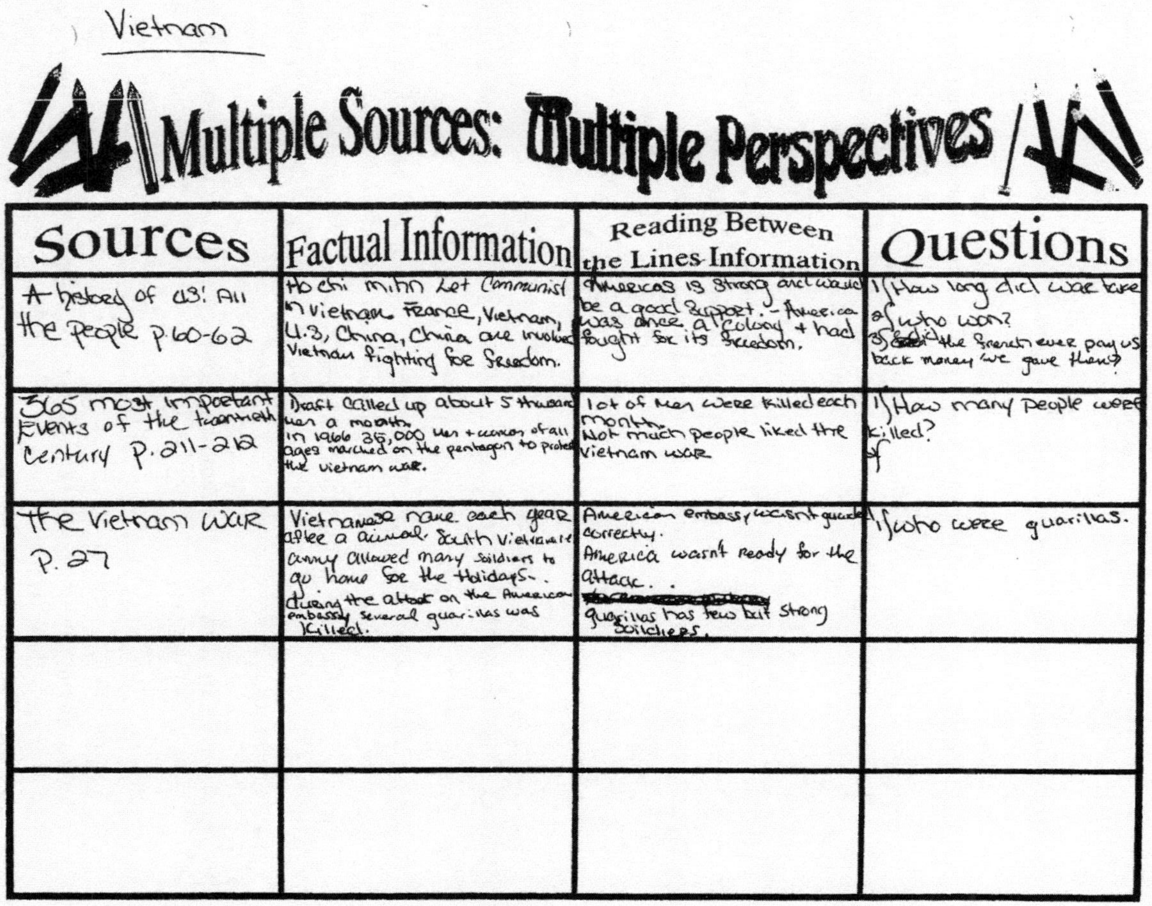

Vietnam

Multiple Sources: Multiple Perspectives

Sources	Factual Information	Reading Between the Lines Information	Questions
A History of US: All the People P.60-63	Ho Chi Minh Let Communist in Vietnam. France, Vietnam, U.S, China, China are involed. Vietnam fighting for freedom.	America is strong and would be a good support. America was once a colony + had fought for its freedom.	1) How long did the war last? 2) Who won? 3) Did the French ever pay us back money we gave them?
365 most important Events of the Twentieth Century P. 211-212	Draft called up about 5 thousand men a month. In 1968 35,000 men + women at all ages marched on the pentagon to protest the vietnam war.	Lot of men were killed each month. Not much people liked the vietnam war.	1) How many people were killed?
The Vietnam War P. 27	Vietnamese have each year after a annual South Vietnam Army allowed many soldiers to go home for the holidays. During the attack on the American embassy several guerrillas was killed.	American embassy wasn't guarded correctly. America wasn't ready for the attack. Guerillas has two hit strong soldiers.	1) Who were guerillas.

Figure 3.6 Multiple Sources Organizer

Then we read a letter from the "Father" of the Navy SEALs and the protesting words of minorities who were drafted, like Muhammad Ali. I asked why the two opinions might have varied so widely, and the kids said the Lieutenant came from a white background , had been trained in "following orders" and though he thought the war was crazy, his devotion to duty came first. They went on to say that minorities were discriminated against here in the U. S. and were against fighting for a country that didn't treat them as equals. Finally, I asked them to write down why it is important to always examine different points of view when studying history. It wasn't a stellar, meaningful lesson, but it helped me see why the form hadn't worked the way I was expecting it to. It wasn't designed to. If my purpose is to have the kids reading to find out different perspectives on an event in history, I need to explicitly state that and make sure I support them by giving them strategies to make that exploration. I can't just expect the graphic organizer to do the work.

In this reflection, Christine has shared a valuable insight about the ways we use activities or graphic organizers to support learning. We have to make sure the activity is not done for the sake of activity; rather, it is crafted to reach the learning goals we have for our students. Christine's students learned a lot about Vietnam and multiple perspectives in the course of these two days. We all learned an important perspective about teaching and learning—you can't have one without the other.

Owning and Translating History

Zemelman, Daniels, and Hyde note that "Social studies are about phenomena to be explored, not just answers to memorize" (1998, 143). Part of owning history is being able to translate history across time and place—imagining yourself in those events or that time or imagining different events, historical figures, or times converging. We found that this kind of activity supported reading history in several ways.

- In order to translate an event from one genre to another, we have to understand the event and the genre.
- Students have to give texts multiple readings in order to keep details accurate in the translation.
- Students have to think critically about the content to make it meaningful when it changes form.
- Students have to use multiple intelligences to represent learning.
- Making connections across time and place helps make history come alive.

Many creative post-reading activities give students the opportunity to extend their thinking about history. The four we have highlighted here all offer students creative avenues for transferring the content knowledge they have gained.

Alphabet Books

Who can resist a great alphabet book? We found that students not only liked reading alphabet books, but also liked presenting material in the form of an alphabet book. The partial alphabet book shown in Figure 3.7 lets us see what this student thinks is important from his study of the American Revolution. If the alphabet book is then extended to a writing assignment in which students have to use their newly created books to outline or summarize the event, students have the advantage of moving between the verbal and the visual to document their learning.

RAFT

RAFT writing (Santa, 1988) provides students with support in reading, writing, and demonstrating knowledge of history. The RAFT acronym stands for role (R), audience (A), format (F), and topic (T). In order to do RAFT writing, students have to think critically about their reading and study in order to take on a new role, match the audience to the role, create a format that would fit that role, and cover specified topics from the content. RAFT writing can be used in any content area with equally delightful results. The RAFT product can be used for assessment, class presentations, or portfolio projects or as a creative response to content.

Using the RAFT graphic organizer (Allen, 2004), Christine's students brainstorm writing possibilities in each of four categories: roles, audiences, formats, and topics to be covered. The RAFT brainstorming represented in Figure 3.8 documents the range of options students generated in relation to their study of the Great Depression.

The creative students imagined many roles they could take as writers, from journalists to people living in Hoovervilles. Those roles gave them an idea of who the audience would be for their writing from each of the role perspectives. They were then able to brainstorm possible writing formats, such as letters, interviews, reports, news articles, and a last will and testament. They agreed that regardless of the role, audience, and format they chose, they would cover the four topic points: living conditions, political climate, causes,

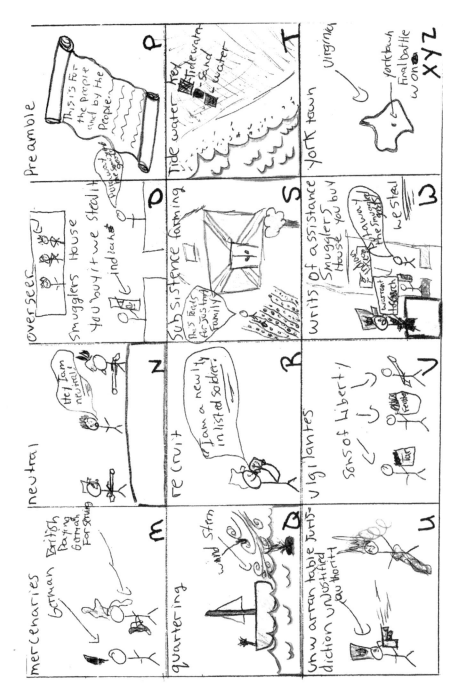

Figure 3.7   Alphabet Book Sample Page

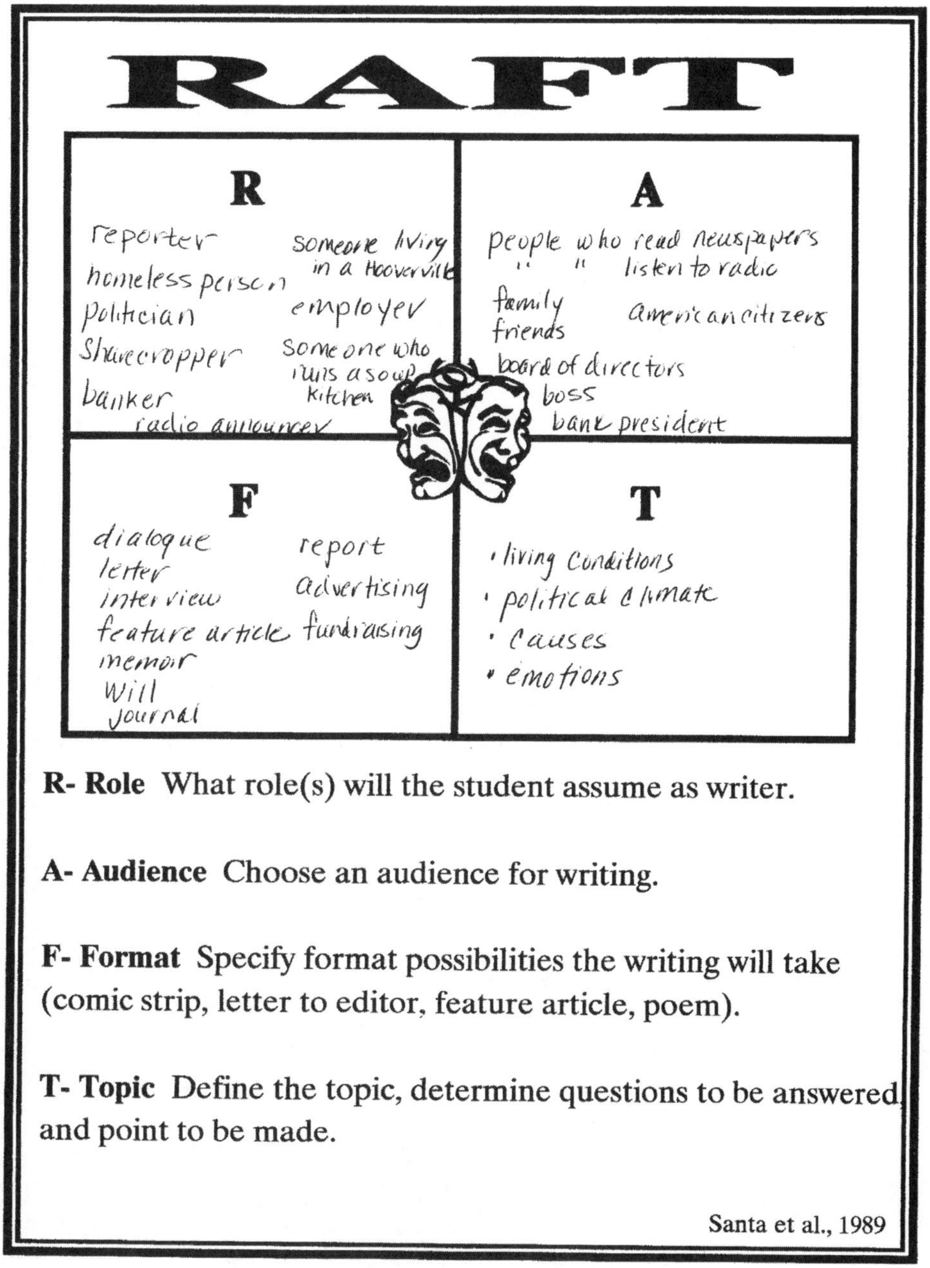

RAFT

R	**A**
reporter someone living in a Hooverville homeless person politician employer Sharecropper Some one who runs a soup kitchen banker radio announcer	people who read newspapers " " listen to radio family American citizens friends board of directors boss bank president
F	**T**
dialogue report letter interview advertising feature article fundraising memoir will journal	• living conditions • political climate • causes • emotions

R- Role What role(s) will the student assume as writer.

A- Audience Choose an audience for writing.

F- Format Specify format possibilities the writing will take (comic strip, letter to editor, feature article, poem).

T- Topic Define the topic, determine questions to be answered, and point to be made.

Santa et al., 1989

Figure 3.8 RAFT Brainstorming Organizer

and related emotions. A sample product from a student who conducted an imaginary interview is shown in Figure 3.9.

SPAWN

SPAWN (Martin, Martin, and O'Brien, 1984) is a reading comprehension and content writing strategy that also gives students the opportunity to move beyond literal-level thinking to larger issues in history. The thinking and writing that SPAWN generates can be a springboard for many other extension and assessment activities. SPAWN is an acronym representing the following writing prompts:

- S—special powers
- P—problem solving
- A—alternative viewpoints
- W—what if
- N—next

Christine used this activity with her students after they read the Christopher Paul Curtis novel *Bud, Not Buddy*, as well as several related readings such as their textbooks and primary source documents. All the readings were connected to a unit Christine had designed, titled "Work and the Depression." She created the SPAWN prompts for small-group discussion followed by individual writing. She used the writing as part of her assessment of her students' understandings of the time period and the events that occurred during that time period. Her SPAWN writing prompts follow:

- S—You have been granted special powers. You use them to stop the stock market crash of October 29, 1929. How is history different because you chose to use your powers in this way?
- P—President Hoover chose to call out the military against the Bonus Army. How would you have solved this problem differently?
- A—You are a journalist traveling around the Hoovervilles in the United States. What kinds of things are you seeing? What are people saying who are living in the Hoovervilles? What are people saying who live in homes and communities surrounding the Hoovervilles?
- W—What if President Hoover had done more to help people during the Depression? How might history have been different?

Hoovervilles

I visited a Hooverville today in Washington D.C. It was very horrible. Although it was placed practically in the "presidents" front yard, he was to busy to notice. This was by far one of the worst I have ever seen. Their were many familys starving and crying babys. One women was giving birth to a baby. But it died soon after birth. There was about 25 familys and about 5 little house that are fit for about 2 familys but each had about 4 familys. The "houses" were very hot and humid. I asked what they ate for breakfast, lunch, and dinner, and they replied, "we only have enough food for one meal a day." I felt very terrible. I got many stories from familys but one inperticular really stood out. It was from a man named Jerry with a daughter named Rya

Figure 3.9

- N—The Dust Bowl has wiped out your family farm. What do you and your family do next?

When students have finished their reading and research, they can work independently or collaboratively to respond to the SPAWN prompts. Discussing the writing tasks with others helps move students from making quick, literal responses to the prompts. The first time you do SPAWN with your students, you should create the prompts. After that, students can create SPAWN prompts for other students or classes. In Christine's class, each student could choose the SPAWN prompt of his choice for his response. The writing in Figure 3.10 shows the creative thinking and content knowledge of this student for the events surrounding the Depression.

Timelines

Timelines can offer us critical historical information not only about historical events, but also about those who created the timelines. Christine and her students use timelines throughout the year. We can see evidence that they thought like middle school historians when she put them to the task of questioning and analyzing timelines. They read and studied the timelines carefully, questioned and discussed aspects of how timelines are created, and even developed their own questions about sociopolitical implications of timelines.

Christine set up their examination of timelines using the timelines on the inside covers of *All the People* (*A History of US*, Book 10), as well as those found in four other textbooks. Students worked in learning groups to compare and contrast the five timelines as well as to ask questions and hypothesize about how the timelines were created. Students were able to find the following points of comparison among the five timelines:

- All have dates or symbols for time.
- All are listed chronologically.
- All are historical and primarily deal with the passage of time in different societies.
- Each major point/event is attached to a specific year.
- They all miss some events.

They also were able to recognize both obvious and subtle differences in the timelines and to synthesize those differences with the following points:

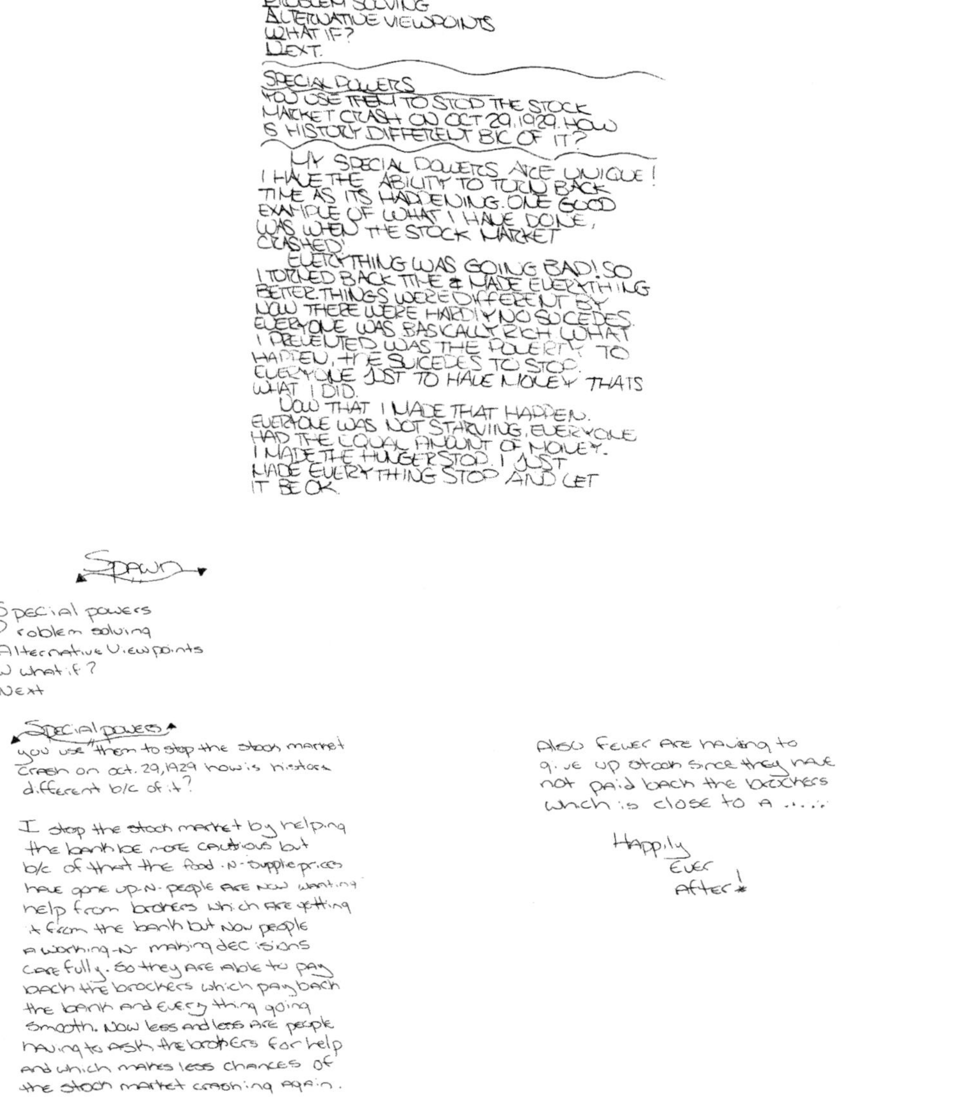

SPAWN
Special Powers
Problem Solving
Alternative Viewpoints
What if?
Next.

SPECIAL POWERS
YOU USE THEM TO STOP THE STOCK
MARKET CRASH ON OCT 29, 1929. HOW
IS HISTORY DIFFERENT B/C OF IT?

MY SPECIAL POWERS ARE UNIQUE!
I HAVE THE ABILITY TO TURN BACK
TIME AS ITS HAPPENING. ONE GOOD
EXAMPLE OF WHAT I HAVE DONE,
WAS WHEN THE STOCK MARKET
CRASHED!
EVERYTHING WAS GOING BAD! SO
I TURNED BACK TIME & MADE EVERYTHING
BETTER. THINGS WERE DIFFERENT BY
NOW THERE WERE HARDLY NO SUICIDES.
EVERYONE WAS BASICALLY RICH. WHAT
I PREVENTED WAS THE POVERTY TO
HAPPEN, THE SUICEDES TO STOP.
EVERYONE JUST TO HAVE MONEY, THATS
WHAT I DID.
NOW THAT I MADE THAT HAPPEN.
EVERYONE WAS NOT STARVING, EVERYONE
HAD THE EQUAL AMOUNT OF MONEY.
I MADE THE HUNGER STOP. I JUST
MADE EVERYTHING STOP AND LET
IT BE OK.

SPAWN
Special powers
Problem solving
Alternative Viewpoints
What if?
Next

SPECIAL POWERS
you use them to stop the stock market
crash on oct. 29, 1929 how is history
different b/c of it?

I stop the stock market by helping
the bank be more cautious but
b/c of that the food -n- supplie prices
have gone up. -n- people are now wanting
help from brothers which are getting
+ from the bank but now people
a working -n- making decisions
carefully. so they are able to pay
back the brothers which pay back
the bank and every thing going
smooth. Now less and less are people
having to ask the brothers for help
and which makes less chances of
the stock market crashing again.

Also fewer are having to
give up stock since they have
not paid back the brothers
which is close to a .....

Happily
Ever
After!

Figure 3.10   Student Writing with SPAWN

- Timelines don't always appear as a line, but sometimes just as a list that is in chronological order.
- The labels B.C. and A.D. are important in some and not others.
- Some show political information, while some focus more on social or cultural information.
- They don't all have titles, which makes some harder to understand when first reading them.

When the groups examined the critical question of how timelines were made, Christine did not give them a lot of guidance, as she wanted to see how well they could apply the big ideas they had talked about in relation to how history is recorded. The points they raised in attempting to answer this critical question demonstrate the high levels of reading history these students have internalized when looking critically at texts.

- Someone had to do research.
- These could have been created by historians, archaeologists, scientists, explorers, or others.
- The information chosen could change, depending on who created the timeline.
- Timelines give us clues to the past.
- The people creating the timeline have to have a broad base of knowledge.
- They must use sources such as books, the Internet, and journals to gather details.
- They must have looked at what people who experienced an important event wrote down.
- Facts have to be straight and to the point.
- They have to pick a time, an area of the world, or a subject as the main focus for the timeline.
- They have to pick events that were important to the time, area, or subject those chose.
- They have to put the things they choose as important into chronological order.

From our perspective, one of the tests of whether or not students can read history is shown when students leave their reading with questions they would still like to answer. When students see the reading of history as not for the purpose of filling in blanks and answering someone else's questions, but as an opportunity to look at multiple sources as a way to generate our own opinions and questions, then I believe our work has had a significant impact. That impact is evident here, as Christine's students are left with many ideas and questions they think are important when reading timelines and prior to creating their own timelines.

- Why doesn't a timeline tell all the facts?
- Where do they really get the information?
- How do the authors know if the information is true?
- What makes something important enough to be included on a timeline?
- Who gets to define the importance of a topic?
- How do they know/remember the exact date an event took place?

In this example, Christine and her students have experienced the joy of reading history to look for big ideas and apply those ideas in their own lives. One of the groups spent significant time just deciding which timeline they liked best and what made that one appealing to them as readers. They decided they liked the timeline in *All the People* the best, because it included things they were interested in such as the miniskirt and the Barbie doll. This led them to conclude that timelines that included modern history made the timeline more interesting. As we examine the timelines these students created using the abilities they had developed to read, research, question, analyze, synthesize, and present in logical formats, we can see the value of supporting the transfer of knowledge rather than the memorization of information (see Figures 3.11 and 3.12).

As we examined their timelines, it was interesting to note how these young historians had no difficulty in matching personal and national/world history. They saw the events in their lives as equally important in their worlds as those that happened on a national level. For example, a move from one home to another is represented with larger print than the Clinton election. This gave Christine a perfect segue back to student questions about how items get represented on a timeline.

Each of the instructional activities helped students make connections between their lives and historical events. As Tarry Lindquist says in *Ways That Work: Putting Social Studies Standards into Practice*, "Learning how to read and reconstruct the past by walking in someone else's shoes helps our kids develop historical perspective" (1997, 101). It is this perspective that helps

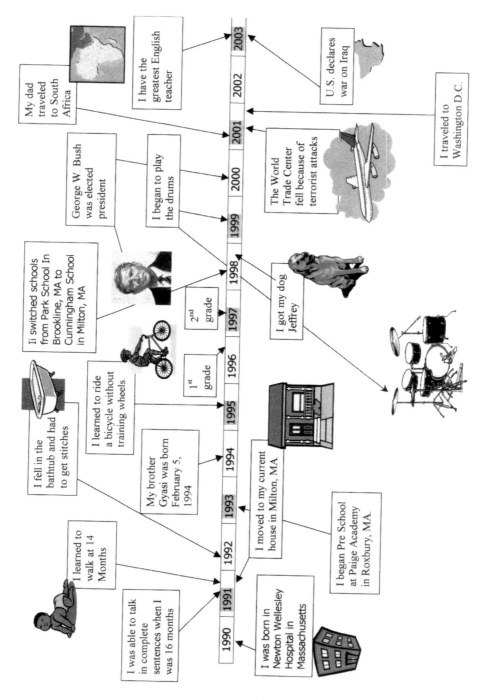

Figure 3.11 Student Timeline

84

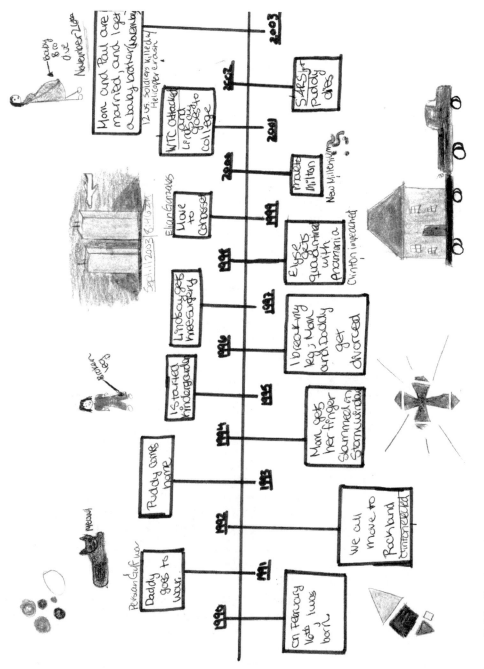

Figure 3.12 Student Timeline

students make a transfer from their class reading and research to other tasks, including the state-mandated test.

Transfer of Knowledge to Testing

But, what about the test? Educators have had to follow mandates that require them to focus on preparing students for standardized tests. This inordinate focus on testing has resulted in a loss of critical instructional practices supporting readers before, during, and after reading history. Neither Christine nor I would ever sacrifice time involving students in engaging activities that make history come alive in order to fill students' heads with discrete bits of information.

I believe there are really only four things we can do to prepare students for any test. First, we have to do everything we can to help make them proficient and critical readers of all types of texts. These pre-, during, and post-reading chapters have offered a variety of instructional strategies for improving students' reading. We have focused on the role of background knowledge, teaching content vocabulary and supporting and monitoring comprehension.

Secondly, we can try to turn students into engaged and interested learners who see reading as a source of information and enjoyment. The more interested students are in learning, the more they will view a test as another learning activity. Some will even try to make the learning activity engaging if they have practiced that approach to overcoming texts that are not interesting to them.

Third, we can teach them strategies for approaching reading challenges. The "how-to" lessons we do with our students when we teach them how to use text supports, how to read a map or a feature article, how to figure out a new or unknown word, or how to compare/contrast or find patterns across texts are their best support when taking a test. If as a teacher you take your state standards and examine the processes in the standards, that will indicate to you the range of instructional strategies you need to teach your students. State standards use verbs to indicate performances expected of students. Each verb (compare, contrast, describe) is a potential strategy lesson.

Finally, we can engage students in the task of decoding the state test so that they understand what will be expected of them. This not only alleviates anxiety about test-taking, but also gives students a high level of self-efficacy. If students believe they have what it takes to be successful and if they know how success will be defined, they are much more likely to be successful.

Christine began the process of helping her students decode the FCAT (Florida's Comprehensive Assessment Test) by dissecting the questions on the practice test. After working in pairs to analyze the questions, students came up with the following question types:

- Definition: used a sentence from the reading that had an "unknown" word in it
- Main Idea: needed to find a main idea for an entire reading as well as just for one paragraph
- Point of View: have to think about what you read and figure out the best answer to fit the author's point of view
- Best Title: have to read something and figure out the best title
- Testing for Facts: have to read something and find the answer to a question

After students deconstructed the kinds of questions they found on the test, they used pages 72–73 in *Liberty for All?* (*A History of US*, Book 5) as the reading sample. They selected the blue box, "The Chinese, the Know-Nothings, and Abraham Lincoln" because of its informational nature and length. Then they worked in discussion groups to write FCAT-type questions. In this way, they experienced the testing process in reverse. The sample student questions shown in Figure 3.13 indicate how well these students now understand the kinds of test questions they will be expected to answer. They are beginning to internalize the language of testing (main idea, most likely, best, point of view, relationship, opinion) and how we go about the task of answering test questions. I'm sure they wouldn't want to do this every day, but the time was well spent both in developing test awareness and also in providing some testing strategies.

Environments That Support Extending and Transferring Content Knowledge

Hillocks has defined "environmental teaching" as

> teaching that creates environments to induce and support active learning of complex strategies that students are not capable of using on their own. It is based on the assumption that teaching need not await development of students for learning to occur, but that in Vygotsky's terms, "learning precedes development." (1995, 55).

Developmentally, many middle school students would not be ready for the kind of learning we have highlighted in this chapter on extending and trans-

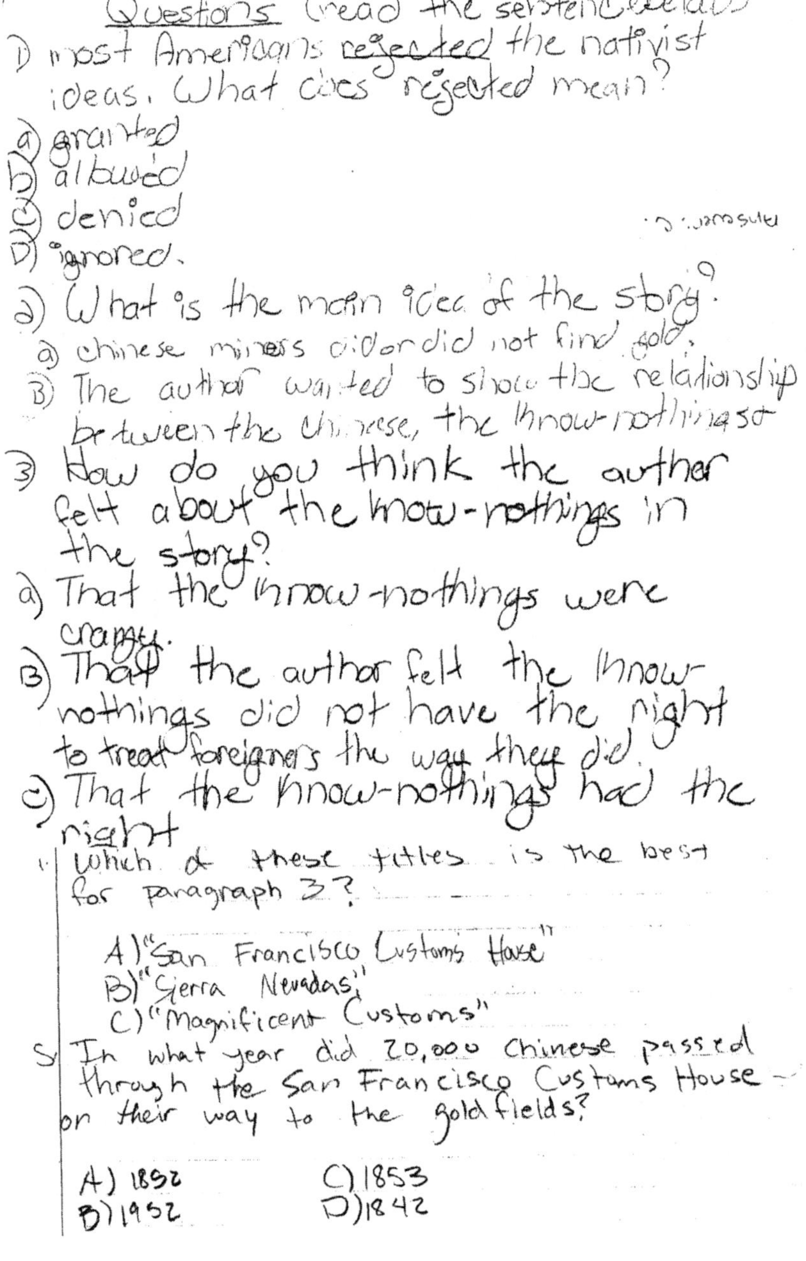

Questions (read the sentence below)
1) most Americans rejected the nativist
ideas. What does rejected mean?

a) granted
b) allowed
c) denied
D) ignored.

2) What is the main idea of the story?
   a) chinese miners did or did not find gold.
   B) The author wanted to show the relationship
      between the chinese, the know-nothings.

3) How do you think the author
   felt about the know-nothings in
   the story?
   a) That the know-nothings were
   crappy.
   B) That the author felt the know-
   nothings did not have the right
   to treat foreigners the way they did.
   c) That the know-nothings had the
   right
   4. Which of these titles is the best
      for paragraph 3?

      A) "San Francisco Customs Have"
      B) "Sierra Nevadas"
      C) "Magnificent Customs"
   5. In what year did 20,000 chinese passed
      through the San Francisco Customs House
      on their way to the gold fields?

      A) 1852   C) 1853
      B) 1952   D) 1842

Figure 3.13 Student-composed Test Questions

ferring content knowledge. Many still enjoy and feel confident answering literal questions and would be overwhelmed with the depth of knowledge and processing required to make such transfers. Environments that support that kind of learning have several characteristics in common:

- The teacher models her learning and gives students the benefit of seeing her missteps.
- The teacher is knowledgeable about a variety of resources that will support student learning and makes those resources available to her students.
- Students know that the only unacceptable learning behavior is not trying. That knowledge is supported by valuing all members of the community.
- The teacher knows how to teach strategies for independent learning.
- The teacher scaffolds the extension and transfer of knowledge in the same way she invites learning.

Students are willing and able to move beyond answering questions each day in their social studies class. Zemelman, Daniels, and Hyde remind us in their *Best Practice* that "Students don't become self-motivated learners by listening to civics lectures for twelve years. They do it by regularly practicing the kind of inquiry, evaluation, decision-making, and action they'll be called upon to exercise later" (1998, 138). Extending and transferring content knowledge should be a common occurrence in our classrooms—planned and supported for academic success.

Chapter 4

Best Practice
in Reading History

Covering less in more depth not only ensures better understanding, but
increases the likelihood that students will pursue future inquiry of their
own at later times.

Zemelman, Daniels and Hyde (1998, 140)

Zemelman, Daniels, and Hyde remind us of the goal that keeps many of us in
education—the hope that we can create independent, self-motivated learners. Moving students from the views of history they hold when they come
into the classroom and to those highlighted in this goal is a monumental
journey. Joel was one of those students who challenged the depth of
Christine's resources in making that journey when he entered her room on
the first day of school last year.

> "I'm allowed to fail one class every year. And, every year, it's history."
> "Welcome to our class. Choose any seat."
> I quickly learned that Joel wasn't kidding. I asked his other teachers and,
> indeed, he had failed history every year. In our first class discussion
> about why we study history, I learned the root of Joel's problem with his-
> tory classes.
> "Come on, Miss. It's not like these are real people or anything. What's the
> point?"

After many frustrating days with the Joels of our classrooms, we all hope
for a comment such as the one Christine finally heard: "Yo, Miss L. History
makes sense to me now. I mean, we can't let anything like this ever happen
again (referring to the Holocaust)."

The essential question for us as teachers is what kind of curriculum, instruction, and assessment will get more students to that goal. Which are the practices we should increase and which are those we should decrease if we want to help a student like Joel move from seeing history as useless and irrelevant to believing that reading history changes our behavior and our world?

Highlighting "Best Practice"

In *What Really Matters for Struggling Readers,* Allington says, "The search for any 'one best way' to teach children is doomed to fail because it is a search for the impossible" (2000, 22). While there may not be any one best way, I do believe there are effective practices that create a foundation of support for making our study and reading of history accessible, informative, and enjoyable.

Increase	Decrease
• Use of supplemental resources, including young adult fiction, nonfiction, informational texts, poetry, periodicals, historical newspapers, and artifacts.	Use of textbook as the sole source of information.
• Use of shared reading as an approach that offers students great access to a common base of knowledge, an opportunity to hear fluent reading, and ideas for independent reading and inquiry.	Use of round-robin reading.
• Use of student questions to inform curriculum and instruction.	Use of questions from the textbook.
• Use of student exploration and inquiry to find meaning from different sources available to them.	Use of transmission model to communicate information.
• Use of student choice of materials for learning.	Use of traditional texts as source of information.
• Use of creative and in-depth word study, with a few key words and concepts forming the basis of the word study	Use of lists of words from a textbook chapter.

- Use of thematic approach to reading history.

  Use of looking at history from only a chronological perspective.

- Use of strategy (how-to) lessons to increase students' abilities to continue learning independently.

  Use of content coverage as the role of teaching.

- Use of reading and writing to help students understand, organize, and remember content.

  Use of weak study techniques.

- Use of graphic organizers and webbing to help make abstract content more accessible and understandable.

  Use of unsupported talk.

- Student talk.

  Teacher talk.

- Alternative ways for students to demonstrate learning.

  Traditional multiple-choice or fill-in-the-blanks tests.

As we all strive to make learning more meaningful and memorable for our students, most of us find ourselves letting go of some practices and adapting some others for a new generation of learners. In *Methods That Matter: Six Structures for Best Practice Classrooms*, Daniels and Bizar highlight the importance of teachers as learners. "Teachers who are learning in their own classrooms are very often working at the edge of their comfort zones in areas where they have not gone before. But by taking this risk, they contribute something rare and vital: direct modeling of how a resourceful and curious adult thinks, how she encounters and deals with new information" (1998, 30).

As curriculum, instruction, and assessment planners in our classrooms and our districts, we ultimately choose how we create a bridge between students' background, attitude, and experiences and the content knowledge and perspectives we want them to gain. In Figure 4.1, I highlight possible ways to make that decision. If we choose what we do in our classrooms only by following mandates, we often ignore the diverse needs and experiences of our learners. For many years, I was in the survivor mode; my goal each day was to find activities that would engage my learners. The danger in planning curriculum in this way is that we can miss critical content and processes in our quest to find yet another great activity.

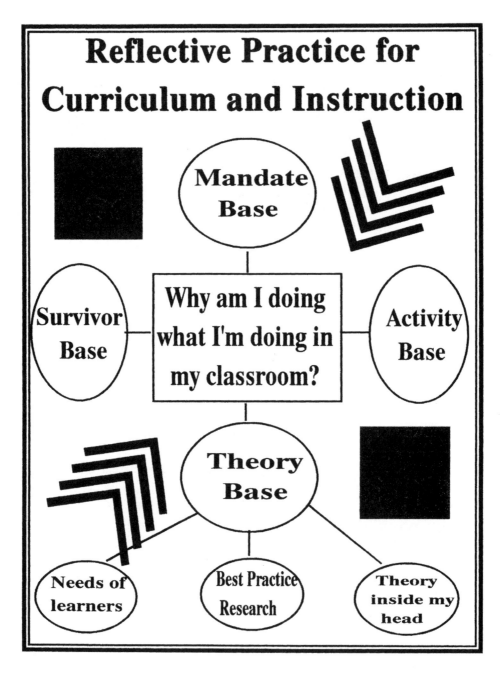

Figure 4.1 Teacher Planning Diagram

I believe the more productive way for us to approach our professional role is from a theory base. When working from a theory base, we are constantly building and refining our theories based on three critical areas: examining the needs of the learners in our classrooms, translating theory into practice, and testing the theories we have inside our heads. These theories may be deeply rooted in our days as students or student teachers. For example, we can hold on to ineffective practices such as having students look up lists of unfamiliar and unrelated words, believing that they are learning vocabulary in the process. It is a theory/belief we have in our heads that came out of our experiences. When we plan curriculum, instruction, and assessment from a theory base, we have become reflective practitioners.

As reflective practitioners, we are constantly assessing the efficacy of our work with our students in five areas: time, choice, resources, support, and connections. We examine the needs of our students, the successes and failures of our plans, and the ways we ask students to demonstrate their learning. We use that information to see which students need more time or more support. We also use that feedback to examine resources to see if we have chosen the most appropriate resources to meet the needs of our students—and we provide them some choice in the resources they use. Finally, we look for ways to make interdisciplinary and life connections, so that students will see learning as meaningful, purposeful, and relevant.

While we may all teach content differently and while we definitely don't share the same students, I believe that both reflective practitioners share subtle and obvious characteristics. Those characteristics set us apart from those who come to school to "cover" a curriculum, because they push us to figure out ways to uncover the curriculum *with* our students. We are the thinkers Daniel Quinn talks about in *My Ishmael, A Sequel: The Phenomenon Continues*:

> "Thinkers aren't limited by what they know, because they can always increase what they know. Rather they're limited by what puzzles them, because there's no way to become curious about something that doesn't puzzle you. If a thing falls outside the range of people's curiosity, then they simply *cannot* make inquiries about it. It constitutes a blind spot— a spot of blindness that you can't even know is there until someone draws your attention to it." (1997, 65)

These "thinkers" are reflective educators who are

- *Learners* who think about why they are doing what they are doing
- *Questioners* who pose questions about their practice and the theory inside their heads

- *Challengers* who push the status quo
- *Builders* of new ways of doing our work
- *Protectors* of effective practices
- *Listeners* who carefully analyze and synthesize new information
- *Experimenters* who are willing to try out new ideas
- *Observers* who "record" findings for reflection and analysis.

Does being a reflective educator make all our students cheerful, active, and passionate readers and learners of history? It would be great if that were true, but our students come to us with diverse needs, and only some of those needs are academic. By using our own strengths as "thinkers" and the instructional strategies we highlight in this text, we gave these students support for reading their school assignments; we also laid foundations that had many of them reading history for pleasure. Those are at least the beginnings of lifelong reading. As we all know, some days that is as good as it gets.

Graphic Organizers
to Support Instruction

The graphic organizers included here support instruction for student thinking and learning. These are organized alphabetically and may be duplicated for use in your classroom

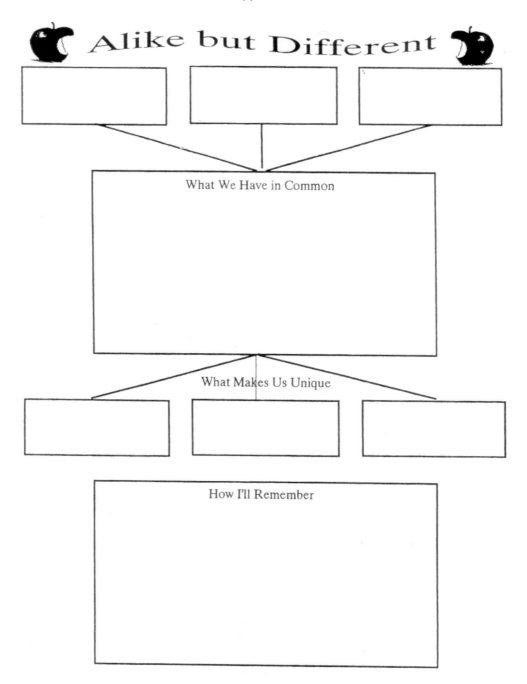

Alike but Different

What We Have in Common

What Makes Us Unique

How I'll Remember

B - K - W - L - Q

Build Background	What do I know?	What do I want to know?	What did I learn?	What new questions do I have?

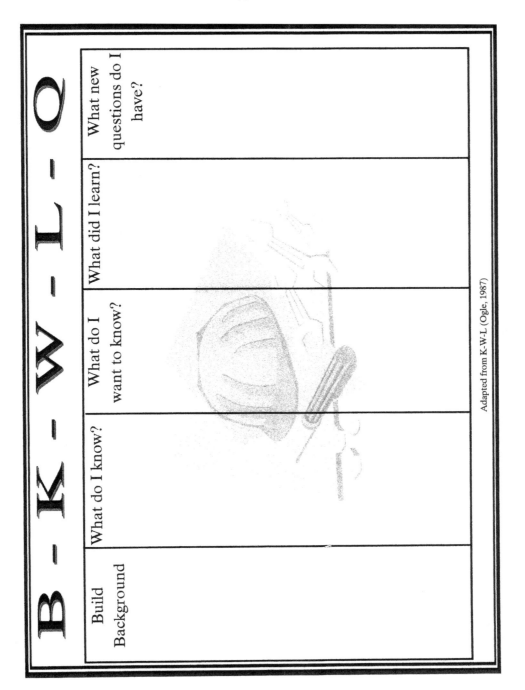

Adapted from K-W-L (Ogle, 1987)

Book Pass

Title	Author	Comment

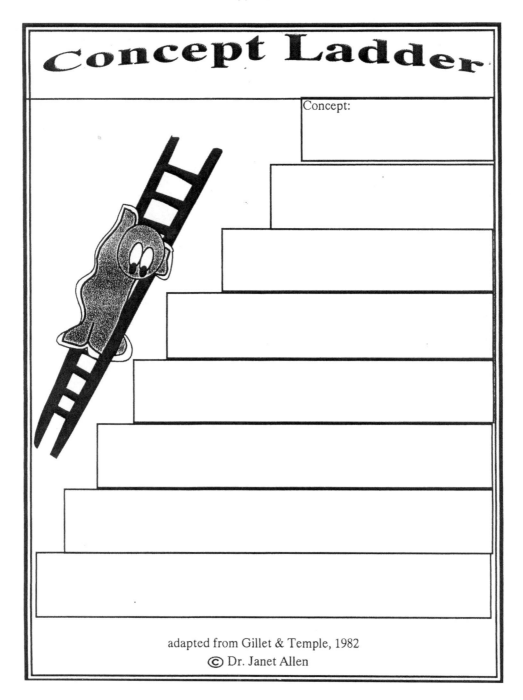

Concept Ladder

Concept:

adapted from Gillet & Temple, 1982

© Dr. Janet Allen

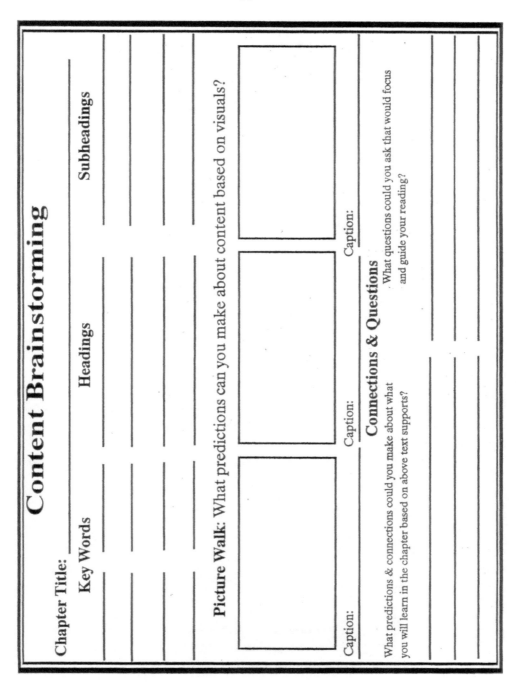

Content Brainstorming

Chapter Title:

Key Words   **Headings**   **Subheadings**

Picture Walk: What predictions can you make about content based on visuals?

Caption: Caption: Caption:

Connections & Questions

What predictions & connections could you make about what you will learn in the chapter based on above text supports?

What questions could you ask that would focus and guide your reading?

Looking At Our Options

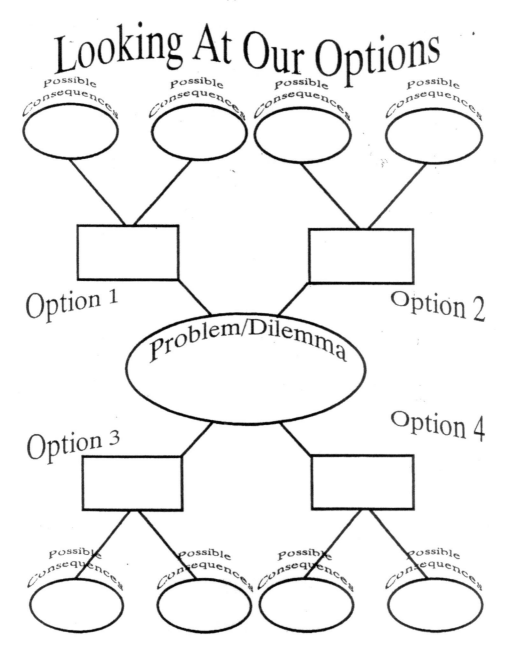

Multiple Sources: Multiple Perspectives

Sources	Factual Information	Reading Between the Lines Information	Questions

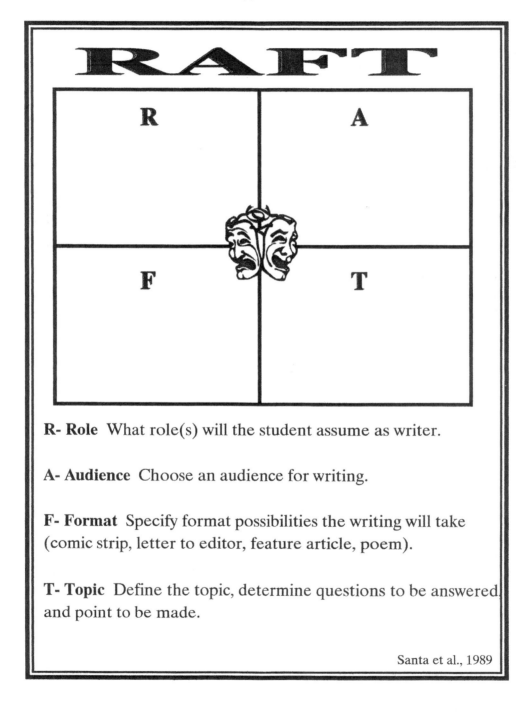

R- Role What role(s) will the student assume as writer.

A- Audience Choose an audience for writing.

F- Format Specify format possibilities the writing will take (comic strip, letter to editor, feature article, poem).

T- Topic Define the topic, determine questions to be answered, and point to be made.

Santa et al., 1989

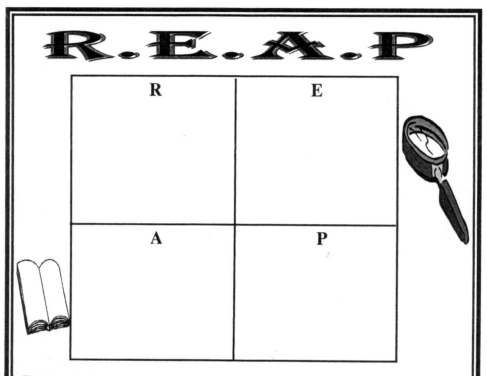

R.E.A.P

R- Read the text. Jot down the title and author.

E- Encode the text by putting the main ideas in your own words/language.

A- Annotate the text by writing a statement that summarizes the important points.

P- Ponder the text by thinking and talking about what you learned. Ask yourself why the author wrote the text. What do you think the author hopes you'll learn?

Eanet & Manzo, 1976

Skimming & Scanning

First Impressions	Fast Facts	"Final Thoughts"
※　　※　　※　　※	※　　※　　※　　※	※　　※　　※　　※

Story (Chapter) Map

Story Map

The setting/main characters
The statement of the problem

Event 1

Event 2

Event 3

Event 4

Event 5

Event 6

Event 7

Statement of the Solution
Story theme (What is the story *really* about?
Values brought out in the story

THINGS WE CAN READ FROM A - Z

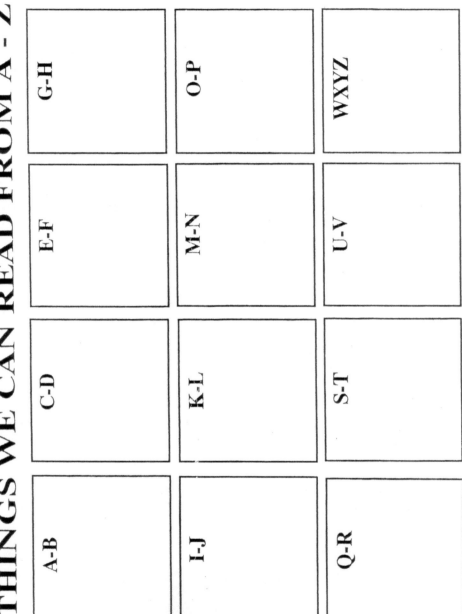

A-B	C-D	E-F	G-H
I-J	K-L	M-N	O-P
Q-R	S-T	U-V	WXYZ

Words in Context

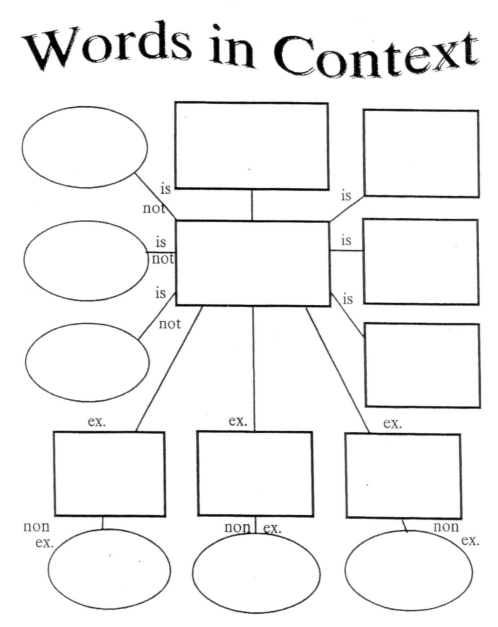

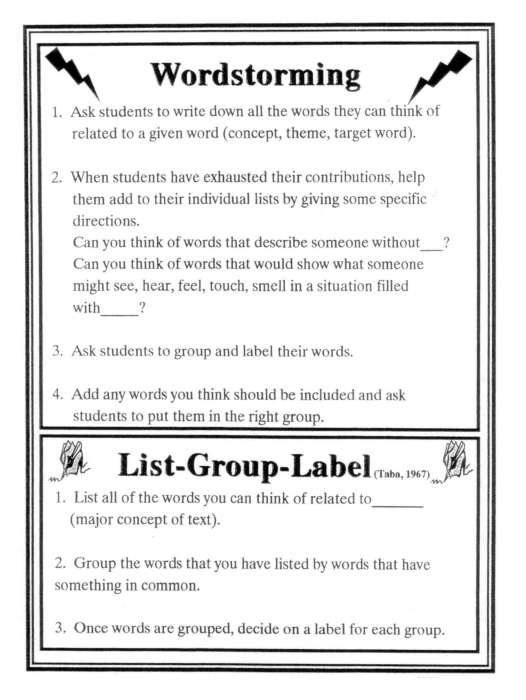

Wordstorming

1. Ask students to write down all the words they can think of related to a given word (concept, theme, target word).

2. When students have exhausted their contributions, help them add to their individual lists by giving some specific directions.
   Can you think of words that describe someone without___?
   Can you think of words that would show what someone might see, hear, feel, touch, smell in a situation filled with_____?

3. Ask students to group and label their words.

4. Add any words you think should be included and ask students to put them in the right group.

List-Group-Label (Taba, 1967)

1. List all of the words you can think of related to_____ (major concept of text).

2. Group the words that you have listed by words that have something in common.

3. Once words are grouped, decide on a label for each group.

Writing To Learn

Source:

Facts:

Response:

Connection:
I wonder:

I want to know:
_____
_____
_____

Source:

Facts:

Response:

Connection:
Now that I know:

I'm interested in knowing:
_____
_____
_____

Source:

Facts:

Response:

Professional Resources for Reading History

Christine has found that many professional books have been helpful for teaching history. Some focus entirely on content literacy, while others focus on reading, writing, and thinking across disciplines. The ones she has annotated here are those she returns to many times throughout the year to refine her thinking and to discover new ideas.

Professional Resources for Reading History

Allen, Janet. (1999). *Words, Words, Words: Teaching Vocabulary in Grades 4–12*, Portland, ME: Stenhouse Publishers. 1-57110-085-7

A fantastic look at vocabulary and how to teach it across the content areas. Packed with good ideas about how to help students truly understand the target words in our disciplines.

Allen, Janet. (2000). *Yellow Brick Roads: Shared and Guided Paths to Independent Reading 4–12*. Portland, ME: Stenhouse Publishers. 1-57110-319-8

Shared and guided reading have played a large part in helping my students connect to the history we are studying. This will help with "how to" tips, resource tips, a general wealth of other knowledge.

Bomer, Randy. (1995). *Time for Meaning: Crafting Literate Lives in Middle and High School*. Portsmouth, NH: Heinemann.

My history classroom is similar to a workshop setting in an English/language arts classroom. This book helped me with ways to implement more writing in that setting.

Brown, Cynthia Stokes. (1994). *Connecting with the Past: History Workshop in Middle and High Schools*. Portsmouth, NH: Heinemann. 0-435-08901-3

A great, short look at what a workshop setting might look like in a history class.

Brown, Jean E. and Elaine C. Stephens. (1995). *Teaching Young Adult Literature: Sharing the Connection*. Belmont, CA: Wadsworth Publishing Company. 0-534-19938-0

Daniels, Harvey, and Marilyn Bizar. (1998). *Methods that Matter: Six Structures for Best Practice Classrooms*. Portland, ME: Stenhouse Publishers.

Broken down by subject matter, with both pedagogical and practical information about implementing what have come to be recognized as universal "best practices" in education.

Edinger, Monica, and Stephanie Fins. (1998). *Far Away and Long Ago: Young Historians in the Classroom.* Portland, ME: Stenhouse Publishers. 1-57110-044-X

Written with the assistance of enthusiastic elementary student "guinea pigs," this book shows how we can bring history to life in our classrooms. It is easily adaptable across grade levels.

Lindquist, Tarry. (1995). *Seeing the Whole through Social Studies.* Portsmouth, NH: Heinemann. 0-435-08902-1

All of her books are written with elementary students in mind, but they are easily applicable and adaptable to other grade levels. I want to be this woman when I grow up. All three of her books have spawned adaptations of her ideas in my classroom. This book was the first social studies professional book that I got my hands on, and it changed the way I saw my subject and the teaching of it.

Lindquist, Tarry. (1997). *Ways that Work: Putting Social Studies Standards into Practice.* Portsmouth, NH: Heinemann. 0-435-08907-2

Lindquist, Tarry, and Douglas Selwyn. (2000). *Social Studies at the Center: Integrating Kids, Content, and Literacy.* Portsmouth, NH: Heinemann. 0-325-00168-5

Harvey, Stephanie. (1998). *Non-Fiction Matters.* Portland, ME: Stenhouse Publishers. 1-57110-072-5

Harvey, Stephanie, and Anne Goudvis. (2000). *Strategies that Work: Teaching Comprehension to Enhance Understanding.* Portland, ME: Stenhouse Publishers.

Both of Harvey's books have provided me with great strategies for finding suitable text and knowing what to do with them when I had them.

Kobrin, David. (1996). *Beyond the Textbook: Teaching History Using Documents and Primary Sources.* Portsmouth, NH: Heinemann. 0-435-08880-7

Primary sources are a buzz topic in education right now. This book is a fantastic, brief look at ways to integrate them.

Lattimer, Heather. (2003). *Thinking through Genre: Units of Study in Reading and Writing Workshops 4–12.* Portland, ME: Stenhouse Publishers. 1-57110-352-X

Many of the genres discussed in this book are perfect for the history classroom, very easily adapted across grades and to your content area.

Loewn, James W. (1995). *Lies My Teacher Told Me: Everything Your American History Textbook Got Wrong.* New York: Simon and Schuster. 0-684-81886-8

Humorous and thought-provoking, I read it for me and enjoy taking snippets into the classroom.

Macrorie, Ken. (1984). *The I-Search Paper: Revised Edition of Searching Writing.* Portsmouth, NH: Boynton/Cook.

Tired of reading research papers that sound like poorly plagiarized versions of *Encyclopedia Britannica*? Give this one a whirl. It will make you and your students view research very differently—less like the enemy.

Romano, Tom. (1987). *Clearing the Way: Working with Teenage Writers.* Portsmouth, NH: Heinemann. 0-435-08439-9

Both of the books that I have read by Romano have had two benefits: I really enjoyed reading them, and they gave me incredible ideas about how to help my students become better writers.

Romano, Tom. (1995). *Writing with Passion.* Portsmouth, NH: Boynton/Cook. 0-86709-362-5

Santa, C. (1998). *Content Reading Including Study Systems Reading, Writing and Studying Across the Curriculum.* Dubuque, IA: Kendall/Hunt.

This one has some good ideas about approaching the reading in a content classroom.

Steffey, Stephanie, and Wendy J. Hood. (1994). *If This Is Social Studies, Why Isn't It Boring?* Portland, ME: Stenhouse Publishers. 1-57110-003-2

Each chapter is by a different author, and each one offers fresh ideas for "getting out of the rut" and helping kids see why social studies can (and should) be interesting.

Tovani, Cris. (2000). *I Read It, But I Don't Get It.* Portland, ME: Stenhouse Publishers. 1-57110-089-X

Along with Janet's books and the books by Stephanie Harvey, Cris's book has helped me look at breaking down the reading task so that kids can understand what good readers do, and what they wind up with when they're done.

Trefil, James, et al., ed. (2002). *The New Dictionary of Cultural Literacy: What Every American Needs to Know.* New York: Houghton Mifflin. 0-61822-647-8

I do not subscribe to the idea that there is a "canon" or knowledge that every American needs to know, but I do know that when I need short snippets of information, this book is very helpful.

Tunnell, Michael O. and Richard Ammon. (1993). *The Story of Ourselves: Teaching History through Children's Literature.* Portsmouth, NH: Heinemann. 0-435-08725-8

A good look at both literature choices and strategies for the history classroom.

Zemelman, Steven, Harvey Daniels, and Arthur Hyde. (1993). *Best Practice.* Portsmouth, NH: Heinemann. 0-435-08788-6

Resources for Reading History

There are many resources, both print and online, that can add rich content and meaningful context for social studies lessons. We have highlighted those resources particularly useful for the instruction described in this book.

Resources for Reading History

Bridges and Borders: Diversity in America
Time, Inc.
Time Education Program
1-800-882-0852

This collection of readings from *Time* magazine from 1923 to 1994 has been invaluable in my classroom. It is worth buying simply for the reprint of the article about the Sunday -school bombing in Birmingham, Alabama.

The Civil War Collection: Artifacts and Memorabilia from the War between the States
Chronicle Books LLC
85 Second Street
San Francisco, CA 94105
http://www.chroniclebooks.com/
"Featuring items from the National Archives and the Museum of the Confederacy"
Text by Bob Zeller
ISBN 0-8118-2644-9

This is truly one of the coolest collection of artifact facsimiles I have ever seen (and the kids agreed with me). The collector/author compiled these documents and photos and provides a guide that explains what is in the box. Also included are translations of the documents that are more difficult to read. There is a clothing catalog (it contains primarily military dress, but also acts as a kind of almanac of information for the year 1863), a letter written by a dying soldier to his father, a letter from a female Confederate spy, and a casualty list for the 54th Regiment Massachusetts Volunteers led by Robert Gould Shaw. There are 24 documents in all. Another amazing collection is a Titanic collection, *Titanic: The Official Story, April 14–15, 1912*. Published by Random House (www.randomhouse.com), it has over 100 pages of "correspondence, government certificates, and contemporary records" dealing with the sinking. The kids love to pore over the deck plans of the ship. ISBN 0-375-50115-0

(The really incredible thing about these two sources? I found them both on the bargain table at a large bookstore chain! They were less than $8.00 each. Ask the information desk at your local bookstore if they can order them.)

Edupress, Inc.
Photo Fun/Photo History Activities
208 Avenida Fabricante, Suite 200
San Clemente, CA 92672-7538
1-800-835-7978
http://www.edupressinc.com/

These packs of photos include activities on the back. The kids love looking at all of the different photos and so on. that go with the topics we are studying. Some of the packs I have used are: Colonial America, Frontier America, Revolutionary War Profiles, The Middle Ages, and China.

Jackdaw Publications
P.O. Box 503
Amawalk, NY 10501
http://www.jackdaw.com/

Documentary Photo Aids
Box 956
Mount Dora, FL 32757

Both of the preceding sources are publishers of primary source documents and photographs; write for a catalog. I have had amazing success using these images and sources to get the kids interested in topics we are studying.

M-C Associates
Dept. R
11910 Lafayette Dr.
Silver Spring, MD 20902
(301) 949-4029

"Pages from Our Past," newspaper reprints; write or call for a catalog. You will be amazed at the amount of time kids will spend poring over these. They get especially involved in calling out the prices of things advertised. "Ms. L! Can you believe eggs were just ten cents?!"

National Council for the Social Studies (NCSS)
8555 Sixteenth Street, Suite 500
Silver Spring, Maryland 20910
(301) 588-1800

NCSS is an incredible resource for social studies and history teachers. The Web site is available to everyone, though there is a member's only section. Check out their position statements and standards for an idea of what is important for students to be able to know and do in relation to these subjects. Each year the council publishes *Notable Social Studies Books for Young People*, a fantastic annotated look at new books in the field. As a member, you also have the option of receiving one of three magazines (or you can pay to receive all) full of ideas and discussions about social studies in the classroom. I have all my back issues and refer to them frequently for ideas.

Old News
Susquehanna Times and Magazine, Inc.
400 Stackstown Road
Marietta, PA 17547-9300
717-426-2212
http://www.oldnewspublishing.com/

This newspaper is published nine times a year. It is full of articles about events, people, and places in history, from the Civil War to whaling ships in the 1800s to the Curies' discovery of new elements. Photos (often primary sources) complement the text. The kids used these like they used *Time for Kids*—as an opportunity for browsing during silent reading. I used them for their great nonfiction articles. They also make a good model for putting together a class newspaper.

Read *Magazine*
Weekly Reader Corporation
3001 Cindel Drive
P.O. Box 8007
Delran, NJ 08075-9978
1-800-446-3355

While it is not their focus, *Read* Magazine often has issues that are based on historical themes. I find them very helpful for alternatives to the textbook. One in particular is an issue on the Harlem Renaissance. We used it for both nonfiction and poetry information during our study on the African-American experience in U.S. History.

Recorded Books, Inc.
270 Skipjack Road
Prince Frederick, MD 20678
1-800-638-1304

Every Wednesday in our class is silent reading day. I faced the same challenges with reluctant readers that the English teacher did, so Janet and I combed the Recorded Books catalog for history-based titles, bought a few sets of headphones (without the radio...)—and silent reading turned around in my class. The company has a fantastic assortment of books to choose from, and it guarantees the tapes.

Steck-Vaughn Company
P.O. Box 26105
Austin, TX 78755
1-800-531-5015
http://www.steck-vaughn.com/

Middle-level teachers and learners will get a lot of use out of series like *Stories of America, Contemporary Biographies, World Myths*, and *The American History Herald* and *The World History Herald* ("newspapers").

These are fantastic sources because they are "short" and so are less intimidating for the students.

Teaching Tolerance
Southern Poverty Law Center
400 Washington Avenue
Montgomery, Alabama 36104
334-264-0286
Fax 334-264-3121
http://www.splcenter.org/

The educational arm of the Southern Poverty Law Center will provide classroom teachers with videos, teaching guides, texts, and posters to help promote cultural awareness and understanding. There are also two teaching kits, *America's Civil Rights Movement* and *The Shadow of Hate.* Fax your request on school letterhead. It is well worth the few minutes it will take to find the letterhead!

Time for Kids
Time and Life Building
1271 Avenue of the Americas
New York, NY 10020-1393
1-800-777-8600

Each article in these magazines is written with students in mind, and the illustrations are eye-catching and informational. My students looked forward to a chance to use these in class, and to browse through them during silent reading. The articles are geared more toward current events, but they provided many connections for us to the history we were studying.

Time Machine: The American History Magazine for Kids
P.O. Box 2879
Clifton, NJ 07015
1-800-742-5402

A magazine full of historical and current events; the articles are accessible for kids, illustrated, and connected to history.

Text Sets That Support Theme-Based Units in History

Listed here are novels, picture books and poetry that can be used as a supplement to the textbook. These text sets are categorized by topic and/or time period. The sets have books at a variety of reading levels which can be used for reading aloud as well as independent reading and research.

Text Sets That Support Theme-Based Units in History

The Colonies, the American Revolution and the New Nation

Anderson, Laurie Halse. (2000). *Fever, 1793*. New York: Scholastic. 0-439-35525-7.

Avi. (1984). *The Fighting Ground*. New York: HarperCollins. 0-06-440185-5

Fleming, Candace. (1998). *The Hatmaker's Sign: A Story by Benjamin Franklin*. New York: Scholastic. 0-439-07179-8

January, Brendan. (1999). *Science in Colonial America*. New York: Grolier. 0-531-15940-X

Katz, Bobbi. (1998). *We the People*. New York: HarperCollins. 0-688-16531-1

Longfellow, Henry Wadsworth. (2001). *The Midnight Ride of Paul Revere*. New York: Handprint Books. 1-929766-13-0 This edition is graved and painted by Christopher Bing. It is beautiful.

Lyons, Mary E. (1997). *The Poison Place*. New York: Simon and Schuster. 0-689-82678-8

McGill, Alice. (1999). *Molly Bannaky*. New York: Houghton Mifflin. 0-395-72287-X (PB)

Pinkney, Andrea Davis. (1994). *Dear Benjamin Banneker*. Orlando, FL: Harcourt Brace. (PB) 0-15-200417-3

Rinaldi, Ann. (1992). *A Break with Charity*. Orlando, FL: Harcourt Brace. (I might use just excerpts from this, depending on the reading level of the kids.)

Small, David. (1994). *George Washington's Cows*. New York: Farrar, Straus, Giroux. 0-374-42534-5

Tunnell, Michael O. (1993). *The Joke's on George*. New York: William Morrow. 0-688-11758-9

Winnick, Karen B. (2000). *Sybil's Night Ride.* Honesdale, PA: Boyds Mills Press. 1-56397-697-8

Slavery and the American Civil War

Adler, David. (1993). *A Picture Book of Frederick Douglass.* New York: Scholastic. 0-439-27617-9

Bunting, Eve. (1996). *The Blue and the Gray.* New York: Scholastic. 0-590-60200-4

Fleischman, Paul. (1995). *Bull Run.* New York: HarperCollins. 0-064-40588-5

Hollander, John. (1999). *War Poems.* New York: Alfred A. Knopf. 0-375-40790-1

Hopkinson, Deborah. (1993). *Sweet Clara and the Freedom Quilt.* New York: Random House. 0-679-82311-5

Katz, Bobbi. (1998). *We the People.* New York: HarperCollins. 0-688-16531-1

Lincoln, Abraham. (1995). *The Gettysburg Address.* New York: Houghton Mifflin. 0-590-93743-X (PB)

Lyons, Mary E., and Muriel M. Branch. (2000). *Dear Ellen Bee: A Civil War Scrapbook of Two Union Spies.* New York: Scholastic. 0-439-34258-9

Polacco, Patricia. (1994). *Pink and Say.* New York: Scholastic. 0-590-54210-9

Ringgold, Faith. (1992). *Aunt Harriet's Underground Railroad in the Sky.* New York: Crown Publishing. (PB) 0-517-58767-X

Rockwell, Anne. (2000). *Only Passing Through: the Story of Sojourner Truth.* New York: Random House. 0-679-89186-2

Sanders, Scott Russell. (1997). *A Place Called Freedom.* New York: Simon and Schuster. 0-689-84001-2

Turner, Ann. (1987). *Nettie's Trip South.* New York: Simon and Schuster. 0-689-80117-3

Winnick, Karen. (1996). *Mr. Lincoln's Whiskers.* Honesdale, PA: Boyds Mills Press. 1-56397-805-9

Winter, Jeannette. (1988). *Follow the Drinking Gourd.* New York: Alfred A. Knopf. 0-679-81997-5s

Minorities and the United States

Looking at Similarities

Altman, Linda Jacobs. (2000). *The Legend of Freedom Hill.* New York: Lee and Low Books. 1-58430-003-5

Bunting, Eve. (1994). *Smoky Night.* Orlando, FL: Harcourt, Brace and Company. 0-15-201884-0

Dooley, Norah. (1996). *Everybody Cooks Rice.* Boston, MA: Houghton Mifflin. 0-395-73233-6

Fleischman, Paul. (1997). *Seedfolks.* New York: HarperCollins. 0-06-027471-9

African Americans

Aliki. (1965). *A Weed is a Flower: The Life of George Washington Carver.* New York: Simon and Schuster. 0-671-66118-3

Altman, Linda Jacobs. (2000). *The Legend of Freedom Hill.* New York: Lee and Low Books. 1-58430-003-5

Bradby, Marie. (1995). *More Than Anything Else.* New York: Scholastic. 0-590-10313-X

Bridges, Ruby. (1999). *Through My Eyes.* New York: Scholastic. 0-590-54630-9

Curtis, Christopher Paul. (1995). *The Watsons Go to Birmingham, 1963.* New York: Scholastic. 0-590-69014-0

Curtis, Christopher Paul. (1999). *Bud, Not Buddy.* New York: Scholastic. 0-439-22188-9

Duncan, Alice Faye. (1995). *The National Civil Rights Museum Celebrates Everyday People.* New York: Troll Medallion. 0-8167-3503-4

Golenbock, Peter. (1990). *Teammates.* Orlando, FL: Harcourt Brace. 0-15-284286-1

Johnston, Tony. (1996). *The Wagon*. New York: William Morrow. 0-688-13457-2

Krisher, Trudy. (1994). *Spite Fences*. New York: Bantam Doubleday Dell. 0-440-22016-5

Krull, Kathleen. (1996). *Wilma Unlimited*. Florida: Harcourt Brace. 0-15-201267-2

Lawrence, Jacob. (1993). *The Great Migration: An American Story*. New York: HarperCollins. Publishers. 0-06-023037-1

Littlesugar, Amy and Floyd Cooper. (2001). *Freedom School, Yes!* New York: Penguin Putnam Books for Young Readers. 0-399-23006-8

Meyer, Carolyn. (1993). *White Lilacs*. Orlando, FL: Harcourt Brace. 0-15-295876-2

Nelson, Marilyn. (2001). *Carver: A Life in Poems*. New York: Scholastic. 0-439-44339-3

Pinkney, Andrea Davis. (1994). *Dear Benjamin Banneker*. Florida: Harcourt Brace. (PB) 0-15-200417-3

——-. (1998). *Duke Ellington*. New York: Hyperion Books for Children. 0-7868-0178-6

Rockwell, Anne. (2000). *Only Passing Through: The Story of Sojourner Truth*. New York: Random House. 0-679-89186-2

Schroeder, Alan. (1989). *Ragtime Tumpie*. Boston, MA: Little, Brown. 0-316-77497-9

Thomas, Joyce Carol. (1998). *I Have Heard of a Land*. New York: HarperCollins. 0-06-023477-6

Williams, Sherley Anne. (1992). *Working Cotton*. Orlando, FL: Harcourt Brace. 0-440-83189-X

Asian Americans

Bercaw, Edna Coe. (2000). *Halmoni's Day*. New York: Dial Books for Young Readers. 0803724446

Bunting, Eve. (1998). *So Far from the Sea*. New York: Houghton Mifflin. 0-395-72095-8

Chinn, Karen. (1995). *Sam and the Lucky Money*. New York: Lee and Low Books. 188000013X

Houston, Jeanne Wakatsuki and James D. (1983). *Farewell to Manzanar: A True Story of Japanese-American Experience during and after the WWII Internment*. New York: Bantam Books. 0553272586

Look, Lenore. (1999). *Love as Strong as Ginger*. New York: Atheneum. 0689812485

Lord, Bette Bao. (1984). *In the Year of the Boar and Jackie Robinson*. New York: HarperCollins. 0-06-44175-8

Mochizuki, Ken. (1993). *Baseball Saved Us*. New York: Lee and Low Books. 1-880000-19-9

Namioka, Lensey. (1999). *Ties That Bind, Ties That Break*. New York: Random House. 0-440-41599-3

Salisbury, Graham. (1994). *Under the Blood Red Sun*. New York: Bantam Doubleday Dell. 0-440-41139-4

Say, Allen. (1993). *Grandfather's Journey*. New York: Houghton Mifflin. 0395570352

————. (1999). *Tea with Milk*. New York: Houghton Mifflin. 0395904951

Uchida, Yoshiko. (1976). *The Bracelet*. New York: Putnam and Grosset. 0-698-11390-X

Hispanic-Americans

Alvarez, Julia. (2001). *How Tia Lola Came to Stay*. New York: Random House. 0-440-41870-4

Buss, Fran Leeper. (1991). *Journey of the Sparrows*. New York: Bantam Doubleday Dell. 0-440-40785-0

Carlson, Lori M., ed. (1994) *Cool Salsa: Bilingual Poems on Growing Up Latino in the United States*. New York: Ballantine Books. 0-449-70436-X

Cisneros, Sandra. (1984). *The House on Mango Street*. New York: Random House. 0-679-73477-5

Cumpian, Carlos. (1994). *Latino Rainbow: Poems about Latin Americans*. Chicago: Children's Press. 0-516-45153-7

Ryan, Pam Munoz. (2000). *Esperanza Rising*. New York: Scholastic. 0-439-12042-X

Native Americans

Bouchard, David. (1997). *The Elders Are Watching*. Vancouver, B.C.: Raincoast Books. 1-55192-110-3

Bruchac, Joseph. (1993). *Fox Song*. New York: Putnam and Grosset. 0-698-11561-9

————. (1993). *The First Strawberries: A Cherokee Story*. New York: Penguin Books USA. 0-8037-1331-2

————. (1994). *A Boy Called Slow*. New York: Putnam & Grosset. 0-399-22692-3

Cohlene, Terri. (1990). *Dancing Drum: A Cherokee Legend*. Vero Beach, FL: Rourke. 0-86593-007-4

Griese, Arnold. (1995). *Anna's Athabaskan Summer*. Honesdale, PA: Boyds Mills Press, Inc. 1-56397-232-8

Hausman, Gerald. (1995). *Coyote Walks on Two Legs: A Book of Navajo Myths and Legends*. New York: Putnam & Grosset. 0-399-22018-6

Hopkins, Lee Bennett, ed. (1999). *Lives: Poems about Famous Americans*. New York: HarperCollins. 0-06-027767-X

Hunter, Sara Hoagland. (1996). *The Unbreakable Code*. Flagstaff, AZ: Northland. 0-87358-638-7

Katz, Bobbi. (1998). *We the People*. New York: HarperCollins. 0-688-16531-1

Koller, Jackie French. (1992). *The Primrose Way*. Orlando, FL: Harcourt Brace. 0-15-200353-3 (This book would be interesting to pair with Ann Rinaldi's *A Break with Charity*, about the Salem Witch Trials in 1692.)

Medearis, Angela Shelf. (1991). *Dancing with the Indians*. New York: Scholastic. 0-590-45982-1

Miles, Miska. (1971). *Annie and the Old One*. Boston, MA: Little, Brown. 0-316-57120-2

Naylor, Phyllis Reynolds. (1973). *To Walk the Sky Path*. New York: Bantam Doubleday Dell. 0-440-40636-6

O'Dell, Scott. (1970). *Sing Down the Moon*. New York: Bantam Doubleday Dell. 0-440-40673-0

Women

Corey, Shana. (2000). *You Forgot Your Skirt, Amelia Bloomer!* New York: Scholastic. 0-439-07820-2

Harness, Cheryl. (2001). *Remember the Ladies: 100 Great American Women*. New York: HarperCollins. 0-688-17017-X

Katz, Bobbi. (1998). *We the People*. New York: HarperCollins. 0-688-16531-1

Krull, Kathleen. (1996). *Wilma Unlimited*. Orlando, FL: Harcourt Brace. 0-15-201267-2

McGill, Alice. (1999). *Molly Bannaky*. New York: Houghton Mifflin. 0-395-72287-X (PB)

Moss, Marissa. (2001). *Brave Harriet: The First Woman to Fly the English Channel*. Orlando, FL:

Harcourt, Brace. 0-15-202380-1

Rockwell, Anne. (2000). *Only Passing Through: The Story of Sojourner Truth*. New York: Random House. 0-679-89186-2

Ryan, Pam Munoz. (1999). *Amelia and Eleanor Go for a Ride*. New York: Scholastic. 0-590-96097-0

San Souci, Robert D. (1995). *Kate Shelley: Bound for Legend*. New York: Penguin Books USA. 0-8037-1289-8

Schlank, Carol H., and Barbara Metzger. (1991). *Elizabeth Cady Stanton: A Biography for Young Children*. Mt. Rainier, MD: Gryphon House. 0-87659-151-9

Yolen, Jane. (1998). *Tea with an Old Dragon: A Story of Sophia Smith, Founder of Smith College.* Honesdale, PA: Boyds Mills Press. 1-56397-657-9

Geography of the United States

Alphabet books published by Sleeping Bear Press (S is for Sunshine, etc.)

Dwyer, Mindy. (1997). *Aurora: A Tale of the Northern Lights.* Portland, OR: Graphic Arts Center. 0-88240-494-6

Hopkins, Lee Bennett, ed. (2000). *My America: A Poetry Atlas of the United States.* New York: Scholastic. 0-439-37290-9

Keller, Laurie. (1998). *The Scrambled States of America.* New York: Henry Holt. 0-8050-5802-8

Loomis, Christine. (2000). *Across America, I Love You.* New York: Hyperion Books for Children. 078680366-5

The Holocaust

Adler, David A. (1987). *The Number on My Grandfather's Arm.* New York: UAHC Press. 0-8074-0328-8

Bachrach, Susan D. (1994). *Tell Them We Remember: The Story of the Holocaust.* New York: Little, Brown. 0-316-69264-6

Deedy, Carmen Agra. (2000). *The Yellow Star: The Legend of King Christian X of Denmark.* Atlanta, Georgia: Peachtree. (PB) 1561452084

Hoestlandt, Jo. (1993). *Star of Fear, Star of Hope.* New York: Scholastic. 0-590-86467-X

Innocenti, Roberto. (1985). *Rose Blanche.* Orlando, FL: Harcourt Brace. 0-15-200917-5 (PB)

Lowry, Lois. (1989). *Number the Stars.* New York: Bantam Doubleday Dell. 0-440-40327-8

Meltzer, Milton. (1976). *Never to Forget: The Jews of the Holocaust.* New York: HarperCollins. 0-06-024174-8

Mochizuki, Ken. (1997). *Passage to Freedom: The Sugihara Story*. New York: Lee and Low Books. 1-880000-49-0

Oppenheim, Shulamith Levey. (1992). *The Lily Cupboard*. New York: HarperCollins. (PB) 0-06-024669-3

Polacco, Patricia. (2000). *The Butterfly*. New York: Penguin Putnam Books for Young Readers. 0-399-23170-6

Rosenberg, Maxine B. (1994). *Hiding to Survive: Stories of Jewish Children Rescued from the Holocaust*. New York: Houghton. 0-395-65014-3

Volavkova, Hana, ed. (1993). *I Never Saw Another Butterfly: Children's Drawings and Poems from Terezin Concentration Camp, 1942–1944*. New York: Random House. 0-8052-1015-6

Wiesel, Elie. (1960). *Night*. New York: Bantam Books. 0-553-27253-5

Zim, Jacob, ed. (1975). *My Shalom, My Peace*. Sonol, Israel: American Israel. 0-07-072826-7

Africa

Bognomo, Joel Eboueme. (1999). *Madoulina: A Girl Who Wanted to Go to School*. Honesdale, PA: Boyds Mills Press. 1-56397-822-9

Brown, Marcia. (1982). *Shadow*. New York: Macmillan. 0-689-71084-4

Feelings, Muriel. (1971). *Moja Means One: Swahili Counting Book*. New York: Puffin Pied Piper. 0-14-054662-6

Gray, Nigel. (1988). *A Country Far Away*. New York: Orchard Books. 0-531-07024-7

Haley, Gail E. (1970). *A Story, A Story*. New York: Troll Associates. (no ISBN available)

Hynson, Colin. (1998). *Great Explorers: Exploration of Africa*. New York: Scholastic. 0-439-15835-4

Kurtz, Jane. (1998). *The Storyteller's Beads*. New York: Scholastic. 0-439-15509-6.

A story of two girls overcoming religious prejudice and famine in 1980's Ethiopia.

Musgrove, Margaret. (1976). *Ashanti to Zulu: African Traditions.* New York: Puffin Pied Piper. 0-14-054604-9

Naidoo, Beverly. (1986). *Journey to Jo'Burg: A South African Story.* New York: HarperCollins. 0-06-440237-1.

Two young children must leave their village near Johannesburg and find their mother in the city. As they travel, they encounter apartheid first hand.

Stanley, Diane. (1994). *Cleopatra.* New York: William Morrow. 0-688-10413-4

India

Demi. (2001). *Ghandi.* New York: Scholastic. 0-439-46962-7

Staples, Suzanne Fisher. (2001). *Shiva's Fire.* New York: HarperCollins. 0-06-440979-1.

Parvati is born during a deadly storm that all but destroys her village. Is it because of this storm that she possesses almost magical powers, including the ability to dance like the Hindu God Shiva?

Whelan, Gloria. (2000). *Homeless Bird.* New York: HarperCollins. 0-06-440819-1.

Through Koly's arranged marriage and subsequent abandonment, we learn about aspects of life in modern India.

Latin America and the Caribbean

Alvarez, Julia. (2002). *Before We Were Free.* New York: Random House 0-375-81544-9

Twelve-year-old Anita and her family live in Trujillo's Dominican Republic, and her father and uncle are involved in the underground movement to overthrow the dictator.

Carlson, Lori M., and Cynthia L. Ventura, eds. (1990). *Where Angels Glide at Dawn: New Stories from Latin America.* New York: HarperCollins. 0-064-40464-1.

Short stories and fables from countries in Latin America.

Dorris, Michael. (1992). *Morning Girl*. New York: Bantam Doubleday Dell. 0-440-83359-0.

Morning Girl and Star Boy are typical siblings; even though they are Taino Indians living in the Caribbean in 1492, modern students will recognize many of their characteristics.

Fine, Edith Hope. (1999). *Under the Lemon Moon*. New York: Lee and Low Books. 1-880000-69-5

George, Jean Craighead. (1989). *Shark beneath the Reef*. New York: HarperCollins. 0-06-440308-4

A great book about choice and confrontation, and a wonderful look at the history and ecology of Baja California.

Gunning, Monica. (1993). *Not a Copper Penny in Me House: Poems from the Caribbean*. Honesdale, PA: Boyds Mills Press. 1-56397-793-1

Joseph, Lynn. (2000). *The Color of My Words*. New York: HarperCollins. 0-06-447204-3.

Twelve-year-old Ana is growing up in the Dominican Republic, learning that words have a power that at the same time can help cause change and help overcome difficulty.

Martel, Cruz. (1996). *Yagua Days*. Boston, MA: Houghton Mifflin. 0-395-73235-2.

Myers, Walter Dean. (1996). *Toussaint L'Ouverture: The Fight for Haiti's Freedom*. New York: Simon and Schuster. 0-689-80126-2

Ryan, Pam Munoz. (2000). *Esperanza Rising*. New York: Scholastic. 0-439-12042-X

Set during the 1920s in Mexico and the United States, we witness Esperanza's transition from a Mexican rancher's daughter to a California field worker.

Thomas, Jane Resh. (1994). *Lights on the River*. New York: Hyperion. 0-7868-1132-3

Yolen, Jane. (1992). *Encounter*. Orlando, FL: Harcourt Brace. 0-15-201389-X

The Middle East

Carmi, Daniella. (1994). *Samir and Yonatan*. New York: Scholastic. 0-439-13523-0

Demi. (2003). *Muhammad*. New York: Simon and Schuster. 0-689-85264-9

Fletcher, Susan. (1998). *Shadow Spinner*. New York: Simon & Schuster. 0-689-83051-3.

Shahrazad has been entertaining the Sultan for almost 1,000 nights, but does not know the end of the story. Can Marjan help her continue, and in the process save the life of the Queen and restore the Sultan's trust in love?

Heide, Florence Parry, and Judith Heide Gilliland. (1990). *The Day of Ahmed's Secret*. New York: William Morrow. 0-688-14023-8

———. (1992). *Sami and the Time of the Troubles*. New York: Clarion Books. (PB) 0-395-72085-0

Nye, Naomi Shihab. (1998). *The Flag of Childhood: Poems from the Middle East*. New York: Simon and Schuster. 0-689-85172-3

———. (1999). *Habibi*. New York: Simon and Schuster. 0689825234 Liyana and her family move to Jerusalem from America, and she experiences what it is to be Palestinian in a place that is fractured by violence.

———. (2002). *19 Varieties of Gazelle: Poems of the Middle East*. New York: HarperCollins. 0060097655.

Staples, Suzanne Fisher. (1991). *Shabanu: Daughter of the Wind*. New York: Random House Publishers. 0679810307.

A growing up story set in the Cholistan Desert in Pakistan. Shabanu is headstrong and independent, but will she be able to choose the course of her own life?

Web Sites to
Support Reading History

Web Sites to Support Reading History

Beacon Learning
http://www.beaconlc.org/

A treasure trove of lesson plans and planning information. You can also submit your successful plans to them.

National Council for the Social Studies
http://www.ncss.org/

A vital link to the pulse of the social studies in the United States. This site has tips, plans, links, bibliographies, and more for the teacher, with additional resources in the "members only" section.

National Council for Teachers of English
http://www.ncte.org/

This is for teachers of English what NCSS is for teachers of social studies. It has the added benefit of being a great site for social studies teachers, too. Good information on using literature in the classroom, Web links, plans, etc.

Rethinking Schools Online: An Urban Education Resource
http://www.rethinkingschools.org/

An online magazine for teachers, covering current trends and issues in education and often highlighting lesson plans to go with current affairs.

The Tallahassee Bus Boycott
http://subvatican.com/boycott/index.html

A great site to incorporate into a unit on Civil Rights.

Quoteland.com
http://www.quoteland.com/

Sorts quotations by topic, theme, author, and so on. Great for looking up quotes that will lead to thought-provoking classroom discussion.

Social Studies Heaven
http://www.salem.k12.va.us/shss/ss/otherhistory.html

This site has links to a multitude of social studies Web sites, from politics to geography games to the History Channel Online.

ERIC Clearinghouse for Social Studies
http://ericso.indiana.edu/

Full of articles, lessons, and contacts for teaching and learning about social studies.

Libertystory.net
www.libertystory.net

"Ideas, people, and events in the history of Liberty." Cicero, Franklin, and Montessori, among many others, can be found here.

Freedom Shrine
http://www.eff.org/Legislation/Freedom_Shrine

A link to documents of freedom from around the world.

AERA SIG: Communication of Research
http://aera-cr.ed.asu.edu/links.html

This is the American Educational Research Association Special Interest Group. It has links to many educational journals.

Animated Atlas
http://www.animatedatlas.com/movie.html

Literally what it says, this animated atlas shows the growth of the United States from 1790 to 1950. The movie lets you pause and click on states and bodies of water to learn further information.

The Best of History Websites
http://www.besthistorysites.net/

This Web site has organized and rated history websites based on "usefulness and accuracy." There is a wealth of connected links here.

Freedom Heroes

http://myhero.com/

A Web site of biographies of men and women around the world who have fought for personal freedoms. It also has excerpts from the writings of children.

Winning the Vote

http://www.winningthevote.org/index.html

A look at the Women's Suffrage Movement.

Women of the West Museum

http://www.wowmuseum.org/

An online look at a museum dedicated to the female experience of the Westward Movement in America.

A More Perfect Union: Japanese Americans and the U.S. Constitution Chinese Exclusion Act 1882

http://www.online.sfsu.edu/~ericmar/catimeline.html

PBS Online

www.pbs.org

PBS not only has incredible educational programs, they also have a fantastic Internet section for teachers. You can explore all grade levels and content areas from their Web site. Many of the preceding sites were found by "surfing" the PBS site.

References

Adler, David A. 1987. *The Number on My Grandfather's Arm.* New York: UAHC Press. 0-8074-0328-8

Allen, J. 2003. *Tools for Content Teaching Content Literacy.* Portland, ME: Stenhouse Publishers.

Allen, J. 2002. *On the Same Page: Shared Reading beyond the Primary Grades.* Portland, ME: Stenhouse Publishers.

Allen, J. 2000. *Yellow Brick Roads: Shared and Guided Paths to Independent Reading 4–12.* Portland, ME: Stenhouse Publishers.

Allen, J. 1999. *Words, Words, Words: Teaching Vocabulary in Grades 4–12.* Portland, ME: Stenhouse Publishers.

Allen, J. 1995. *It's Never Too Late: Leading Adolescents to Lifelong Literacy.* Portsmouth, NH: Heinemann.

Allen, J., and K. Gonzalez. 1998. *There's Room for Me Here: Literacy Workshop in the Middle School.* Portland, ME: Stenhouse Publishers.

Allington, R. 2001. *What Really Matters for Struggling Readers: Designing Research-Based Programs.* New York: Addison Wesley Longman.

Allington, R., and P. Johnston. 2002. *Reading to Learn.* New York: Guilford Press.

Anderson, R. C., E. H. Hiebert, J. A. Scott, and I. A. G. Wilkinson. 1985. *Becoming a Nation of Readers: The Report of the Commission on Reading.* Urbana, IL: Center for the Study of Reading.

Applebee, Joyce, et. Al. 1998. *The American Journey.* Westerville, OH: McGraw-Hill Companies. 0-02-823218-6

Baker, S. K., D. C. Simmons, and E. J. Kameenui. 1995. *Vocabulary Acquisitions: Curricular and Instructional Implications for Diverse Learners.* Technical Report No. 13. University of Oregon: National Center to Improve the Tools for Educators.

Baumann, J.F. and E.J. Kameenui. 1991. *Research on Vocabulary Instruction: Ode to Voltaire.* In Handbook of Research on Teaching the English Language Arts, ed. J. Flood, J.M. Jensen, D. Lapp, and J.R. Squire. New York: Macmillan.

Blachowicz, C. L. Z. 1986. "Making Connections: Alternatives to the Vocabulary Notebook." *Journal of Reading* 29 (2): 43–49.

Blachowicz, C., and D. Ogle. 2001. *Reading Comprehension: Strategies for Independent Learners.* New York: Guilford Press.

Britton, J. 1970. *Language and Learning: The Importance of Speech in Children's Development.* New York: Penguin Press.

Carr, E., and D. Ogle. 1987. "K-W-L Plus: A Strategy for Comprehension and Summarization." *Journal of Reading* 30: 626–31.

Carter, C., and Z. M. Rashkis, eds. 1980. *Ideas for Teaching English in the Junior High and Middle School.* Urbana, IL: National Council of Teachers of English.

Chambers, A. 1996. *Tell Me: Children, Reading and Talk.* Portland, ME: Stenhouse.

Costa, A. L., and B. Kallick, eds. 2000. *Assessing and Reporting on Habits of Mind.* Alexandria, VA: ASCD.

Curtis, C.P. 1999. *Bud, Not Buddy.* New York: Delacorte Press.

Daniels, H., and M. Bizar. 1998. *Methods that Matter: Six Structures for Best Practice Classrooms.* Portland, ME: Stenhouse Publishers.

Davey, B. 1986, *Using Textbooks Activity Guides to Help Students Learn from Textbooks.* Journal of Reading 29: 489–94.

Diaz-Rubin, C. 1996. "Reading Interests of High School Students." *Reading Improvement,* 33 3: 169–75.

Eanet, M., and A. Manzo. 1976. "R.E.A.P.—A Strategy for Improving Reading/Writing Study Skills." *Journal of Reading* 19: 647–52.

Farr, R. 2003. "Building Useful Instructional Reading Assessments." *The NERA Journal,* 39 (1).

Fielding, L. C., P. T. Wilson, and R. C. Anderson. 1986. "A New Focus on Free Reading: The Role of Trade Books in Reading Instruction." In *Contexts of Literacy,* ed. T. E. Raphael and R. Reynolds. New York: Longman.

Flood, J., D. Lapp, and K. Wood. 1992. *Guiding Readers through Text: A Review of Study Guides.* Newark, DE: International Reading Association.

Freebody, P., and A. Luke. 1990. "Literacy Debates and Demand in Cultural Context." *Prospect* 5 (3): 7–16.

Gallagher, M.C., and P.D. Pearson. 1983. "The Instruction of Reading Comprehension." *Contemporary Educational Psychology* 8: 317–44.

Gillet, J.W. C. Temple. 1982. *Understanding Reading Problems: Assessment and Instruction.* Boston: Little, Brown.

Graves, M., and B. Graves. 1994. *Scaffolding Reading Experiences: Designs for Student Success.* Norwood, MA: Christopher Gordon.

Guthrie, J. T., S. Alao, and J. M. Rinehart. 1997. "Engagement in Reading for Young Adolescents." *Journal of Adolescent and Adult Literacy* 40 (6).

Hakim, J. 1993. *A History of US.* New York: Oxford University Press.

Hillocks, G. 1995. *Teaching Writing as Reflective Practice.* New York: Teachers College Press.

Holbrook, S. 1998. "Naked." In *Chicks Up Front.* Cleveland, OH: Cleveland State University Poetry Center.

Kirby, D., T. Liner, and R. Vinz. 1988. *Inside Out: Developmental Strategies for Teaching Writing,* 2d ed. Portsmuth, NH: Heinemann-Boynton/Cook.

Lasky, K. 1994. *Beyond the Burning Time.* New York: Blue Sky Press/ Scholastic.

Lindquist, T. 1997. *Ways That Work: Putting Social Studies Standards into Practice.* Portsmouth, NH: Heinemann.

Lindquist, T., and D. Selwyn. 2000. *Social Studies at the Center: Integrating Kids, Content, and Literacy.* Portsmouth, NH: Heinemann.

Manzo, A. 1969. "The ReQuest Procedure." *Journal of Reading* 13: 23–26.

Martin, C. E., M. A. Martin, and D. G. O'Brien. 1984. "Spawning Ideas for Writing in the Content Areas." *Reading World* 11: 11–15.

McGinley, W., and P. Denner. 1987. "Story Impressions: A Prereading/Writing Activity." *Journal of Reading* 31: 248–53.

McKenna, M. D., D. Kear, and R. A. Randolph. 1995. "Children's Attitudes toward Reading: A National Survey." *Reading Research Quarterly,* 30.

McKeown, M., I. Beck, G. Sinatra, and J. Loxterman. 1992. "The Contribution of Prior Knowledge and Coherent Text to Comprehension". *Reading Research Quarterly,* 27: 79–93.

Nagy, W. 1988. *Teaching Vocabulary to Improve Reading Comprehension.* Newark, DE: International Reading Association.

Newman, F. M. 1988. "Can Depth Replace Coverage in High School Curriculum?" *Phi Delta Kappan*

Ogle, D. 1986. "K-W-L: A Teaching Model That Develops Active Reading of Expository Text." *Reading Teacher* 39: 563–70.

Ohanian, S. 2001. Caught in the Middle: Nonstandard Kids and a Killing Curriculum. Portsmouth, NH: Heinemann, 2001.

Pearson, P. D., and B. Taylor, eds. 2002. *Teaching Reading: Effective Schools, Accomplished Teachers.* Mahwah, NJ: Lawrence Erlbaum.

Quinn, D. 1997. *My Ishmael, A Sequel: The Phenomenon Continues.* New York: Bantam Books.

Readence, J. E., T. W. Bean, and R. S. Baldwin. 1985. *Content-Area Reading: An Integrated Approach,* 2d ed. Dubuque, IA: Kendall/Hunt.

Salisbury, Graham. 1994. *Under the Blood Red Sun.* New York: Bantam Doubleday Dell. 0-440-41139-4.

Santa, C. 1988. *Content Reading Including Study Systems.* Dubuque, IA: Kendall/Hunt.

Schneider, Donald, et. Al. 1994. *Expectations of Excellence: Curriculum Standards for Social Studies.* Silver Springs, MD: National Council for the Social Studies. 0-87986-065-0

Taba, H. 1967. *Teacher's Handbook for Elementary Social Studies.* Reading, MA: Addison-Wesley.

Tierney, R. J., and T. Shanahan. 1991. "Research on the Reading-Writing Relationship: Interactions, Transactions and Outcomes." In Handbook of Reading Research, vol. 2, ed. Barr, Kamil, Mosentha, and Pearson. White Plains, NY: Longman.

Vacca, R. T. 2000. "Taking the Mystery out of Content Area Literacy." In M. McLaughlin and M. Vogt. Creativity and Innovation in Content Area Teaching, ed. Norwood, MA: Christopher-Gordon.

van den Broek, P. & K. E. Kremer. 2000. "The Mind in Action: What It Means to Comprehend during Reading." In *Reading for Meaning: Fostering Comprehension in the Middle Grades,* ed. B. M. Taylor, M. F. Graves, and P. van den Broek. New York: Teachers College Press.

Vygotsky, L. 1962. *Thought and Language.* Cambridge, MA: M.I.T. Press.

Wallis, C. 1998. "How to Make a Better Student." *Time*, October 19, 1998, 78–86.

Zemelman, S., H. Daniels, and A. Hyde. 1998/1993. *Best Practice: New Standards for Teaching and Learning in America's Schools.* Portsmouth, NH: Heinemann.

Index

('i' indicates an illustration)